DWIGHT DAVID EISENHOWER

MARIAN G. CANNON

DWIGHT DAVID EISENHOWER

WAR HERO AND PRESIDENT

Franklin Watts ★ An Impact Biography
New York ★ London ★ Toronto ★ Sydney ★ 1990

Map by: Joe Le Monnier

Photographs courtesy of: Dwight D. Eisenhower Library,
except the following: Associated Press: p. 73;
U.S. Air Force: p. 78; U.S. Army: pp. 103, 116;
National Park Service: p. 139 (both).

Library of Congress Cataloging-in-Publication Data

Cannon, Marian G.
Dwight David Eisenhower : war hero and president / by Marian G. Cannon.
p.   cm. — (An Impact biography)
Includes bibliographical references.
Summary: A biography of the commander general of the Allied forces
in Europe during World War II who became the thirty-fourth President
of the United States.
ISBN 0-531-10915-1
1. Eisenhower, Dwight D. (Dwight David), 1890–1969—Juvenile
literature.   2. Presidents—United States—Biography—Juvenile
literature.   3. Generals—United States—Biography—Juvenile
literature.   4. United States.   Army—Biography—Juvenile
literature.   [1. Eisenhower, Dwight D. (Dwight David), 1890–1969.
2. Presidents.   3. Generals.]   I. Title.
E836.C36   1990
973.921′092—dc20
[B]   [92]   89-24791   CIP   AC

This book is dedicated to my
husband, Jim, for his invaluable
help and encouragement,
and to Kyle, Griff, and Tyler,
in hopes that they may grow up
in a peaceful world

ACKNOWLEDGEMENTS

I wish to thank the many people who helped in the preparation and completion of this book. It was a privilege to have been able to do much of my research at the Huntington Library in San Marino, California, and I wish to thank the Readers' Services Department for their interest and assistance. I also wish to thank the staff at the Dwight D. Eisenhower Library in Abilene, Kansas, for their help and cooperation in securing pictures.

In addition, I am grateful to Gloria Miklowitz, my advisor and friend, who first suggested that I attempt writing this biography, and also to my editor, Iris Rosoff.

Lastly, I would like to thank my family, especially my husband, Jim, who advised and encouraged me, and my young people, Linda, Fred, Jean, and Scott, who were most supportive.

I would like to express one regret. Due to the length and scope of this book, I was unable to mention many of the important American and British military personnel who so greatly helped General Eisenhower win the war in Europe.

CONTENTS

DWIGHT DAVID EISENHOWER

CHAPTER ONE

"If We Were Poor...
We Were Unaware of It"

As General Eisenhower entered a crowded office in Portsmouth, England, early on the morning of June 5, 1944, the assembled Allied generals and admirals fell silent. It was just before D-Day during World War II, the day the Allied forces intended to strike the Nazis on the French coast. General Ike, as supreme allied commander, had to give the final order to attack.

General Eisenhower and the Allied high command had been planning D-Day for many months. Ike had already postponed the Allied landing once because of gale force winds. Now, he knew that the decision to strike was his alone. Hundreds of thousands of lives were at stake; the Allies had to defeat the Nazis immediately or all of Europe would be lost to Hitler.

General Ike looked at the officers gathered in that small room and simply said, "Okay. We'll go."[1]

These few words set in motion the greatest military invasion the world had ever known: the Allied invasion on the Normandy beaches. Ike was willing to make this momentous decision, although he knew that he alone would take either the credit or the blame for the success or failure

General Dwight D. Eisenhower,
Supreme Allied Commander

of this mission. He was confident, but by no means sure, that the Allies would succeed.

Eisenhower was a man with a broad grin and a firm handshake, a man whose friends included President Franklin D. Roosevelt, British Prime Minister Winston Churchill, and thousands of American soldiers. All these people believed that General Ike would win the war for the Allies in Europe. In fact, just before D-Day, Prime Minister Churchill remarked, "There is complete confidence in the Supreme Commander, General Eisenhower."[2]

★ ★ ★ ★ ★

Dwight David Eisenhower attained the high positions of five-star general and president of the United States not by chance, but through perseverance and hard work. Throughout his life he faced challenges head on, took responsibility for his own decisions, and usually reached his goals. Undoubtedly, Ike's early years prepared him for leadership, because his parents gave him a sense of responsibility and a desire to achieve.

Dwight David Eisenhower was born on October 14, 1890, in Denison, Texas, the third son of Ida and David Eisenhower. His father was descended from Swiss-German ancestors who had arrived in the United States in 1741 on the ship *Europa,* and settled in Pennsylvania. Both David and Ida's parents had moved to Kansas in the 1880s with a religious Mennonite group called the River Brethren.

Ida and David met while attending Lane University in Kansas. David had studied engineering, and Ida planned to become a schoolteacher. After they were married, the couple moved to Hope, Kansas, where David opened a general store. However, times were hard, and David's store failed. With their two sons, the couple moved to Denison, Texas, where Dwight was born.

When Dwight was a year old, his family moved again, this time to Abilene, Kansas, a town located in the bull's-eye center of the United States. At one time, Abilene had been a wild west cow town at the northern end of the Chisholm trail, an early route on which cattle were driven north from Texas. At that time it was a rough place, known for gambling, street fights, and occasional Indian raids. Later, after Marshal Wild Bill Hickok took charge, Abilene became a law-abiding community.

During Ike's youth, Abilene was a quiet little town with unpaved streets, where farmers and shopkeepers lived peacefully. In spite of this quiet atmosphere, Abilene still retained a slight flavor of its earlier wilder days.

Ike once said of Abilene, ". . . meet anyone face to face with whom you disagree."[3] Ike lived by this motto all of his life.

Dwight grew up in a two-story frame house behind the Lincoln School on Southeast Fourth Street. His father supported the family by working as an engineer at the Belle Springs Creamery. His mother had her hands full managing their home and six lively sons. From an early age, Ike learned to get along with his brothers, but he also managed to stand up for his own rights. His two older brothers were Arthur and Edgar; the younger ones were Roy, Earl, and Milton. Another son, Paul, died as an infant. Of the six surviving sons, Arthur, Roy, and Milton were usually quiet and serious, while Edgar, Dwight, and Earl were outgoing and at times hot tempered.

From the time they were toddlers, Dwight and his brother Edgar, two years older, were best buddies. They played together constantly. When they attended grade school, the two boys were both nicknamed "Ike," because their last name was so long. Edgar was known as "Big Ike," Dwight as "Little Ike." Later in high school, Dwight dropped the little and was called merely Ike. Although at one time he preferred the name Dwight, somehow the nickname Ike stuck.

One of Dwight's earliest memories was a visit to his Aunt Minnie and Uncle Luther's farm in Topeka, Kansas, just before his fifth birthday. His uncle kept a pair of large geese in the backyard, and every time Dwight went out to play, the big gander squawked and nipped at him, which made him run back in the house in tears.

Finally, Uncle Luther decided that the boy must learn to stand up to the big birds. He gave Dwight an old broom, which had been cut down to child size, and told him that the next time the geese chased him, he should run after them brandishing the makeshift weapon. Dwight took his uncle's advice. Before long, he happily ran after the geese, knowing he was the boss of the backyard.

Ike later said that this episode taught him a valuable lesson: ". . . never to negotiate with an adversary except from a position of strength."[4]

Ike's parents brought up their boys to be hardworking, honest young men. Ike said, "Father was the breadwinner, Supreme Court, and Lord High Executioner. Mother was tutor and manager of our household."[5]

As a young boy, Dwight learned the value of hard work, because all six boys had chores to do around the farmhouse. They took turns sweeping and mopping the floors, feeding the chickens, and milking the two cows. These tasks were rotated regularly, so each boy could experience all the work. After finishing their chores, the brothers had a chance to ride one of the two family horses. The boys completed their work in record time, so each could have his turn.

In addition to their chores, David Eisenhower gave each son a small plot of ground in which to plant vegetables to sell for spending money. Dwight and Edgar grew tomatoes, cucumbers, and sweet corn on their plots. After these were harvested, the two brothers packed the vegetables in their little red wagon and took them to the north side of town where the wealthier people lived. Dwight enjoyed ringing the doorbells and hawking their produce. The boys were happy to make a profit on this venture, for it was their only spending money.

Although all the Eisenhower boys worked hard, Ike never felt that his family was underprivileged. He wrote, "If we were poor—and I'm not sure that we were by the standards of the day—we were unaware of it. All in all, we were a cheerful and a vital family. We would have been insulted had anyone offered us charity; instead my mother was always ready to take home remedies or food and start out to help the sick. The daily prayers included a plea for the hungry. . . ."[6]

Ida and David Eisenhower, being very religious, insisted that their sons go to church and study the Bible. The whole family belonged to the River Brethren Church, which firmly believed in the pacifist philosophy of turning the other cheek. The church members did not believe in any type of fighting, and many refused to go into the armed services. The Eisenhowers were very active in this church, and Dwight's grandfather was the minister of the local River Brethren.

Besides attending church regularly, the Eisenhower family held daily Bible reading sessions in the parlor beside the ebony upright piano which Ida had purchased with her dowry money. Each family member took turns reading the Bible. Ike said that if one of the boys mispronounced a word, he lost his turn and another would take over. Ike tried hard to read well, because he hated to lose his chance to perform. After the Bible lessons and prayers, Ida gave her sons piano lessons, which most of them enjoyed more than the Bible study.

As a young boy, Ike learned to stand up for himself. He and Edgar loved to wrestle with each other, and later Ike began to have fist fights with other boys. Though this behavior was against his parent's wishes, his mother realized that quarreling was part of growing up. Ike's brother Milton said that one day his brothers "got into a lively fight in the house and a neighbor who was there tried to intervene. . . . Mother, without even looking at the two sons, said to the neighbor, 'Let them alone. Let them solve their own problems and things will be better.' "7

At school, Ike soon earned a reputation as a fighter. One reason was that the rivalry between the north side and south side of town promoted a spirit of conflict. In junior high and high school, the children from the north side, the more affluent neighborhood, and the south side, the poorer area, all attended the same schools. After classes were dismissed, fights often occurred between the opposing groups. Ike was one of the ringleaders of the south side.

But as he grew older, the fights became less frequent. At age thirteen, Ike had his last memorable fight with a boy named Wesley Merrifield. Although Ike knew that Wes outweighed him and was faster, he refused to give up. After almost two hours of hard wrestling, Wes said, "I can't lick you, Ike." Ike replied, "Well, Wes, I haven't licked you."8 The badly bruised boys finally gave up and went home to face their angry parents.

Remembering his boyhood fights, Ike said, ". . . Fighting and wrestling were standard games. They were pitting . . . strength and skill against each other in a competitive spirit."9

By the time Ike entered high school, he realized that fist fighting was a waste of time and energy. He decided to use his vitality in a more positive way, by going out for sports.

In high school, Ike was overjoyed when he was se-lected to play on both the football and baseball teams. By the time he was a senior, Ike and his brother Edgar were stars on the same football team. In fact, the brothers were in the same senior class, because illness had kept Edgar out of school for a year.

Ike once said that playing on the football team was a wonderful experience. "I believe that football . . . tends to instill in men the feeling that victory comes through hard—almost slavish—work. . . ."[10]

During the time Ike was on the football team, he had an unfortunate experience. One day he was running up a wooden ramp after a game. He tripped, fell, and scratched his leg badly. The next day, he tried to go back to school, but the wound had caused blood poisoning, and he soon developed a high fever. His parents called the family doc-tor, who gave him medication. In spite of the medicine, the fever persisted, and the doctor considered amputating Ike's leg.

When Ike heard this terrible news, he pleaded with Edgar to keep watch at the door in case he fell into a coma. He begged his brother not to let the doctor cut off his leg. He told Edgar, "I'd rather be dead than crippled, and not able to play ball."[11]

Edgar kept his promise and stood guard over Ike for two days and nights, as the whole family prayed for him. Fortunately, Ike's leg improved, and after he recovered, he was able to play on the football team again.

Every summer, Ike and Edgar loved to go camping and fishing with their friends and faithful dog, Flip, in the woods near the Smoky Hill River, not far from Abilene. Outdoors, they felt free from the pressures of schoolwork and their parents' demands.

Although Ike enjoyed summer the most, he and his pals had time for outdoor adventures in all seasons. In May

*Ike realized his competitive spirit was best used on
the ball field. Here he is with the rest of the Abilene
High School baseball team (top row, second from right).*

1903, the torrential rains that flooded the town of Abilene provided the perfect opportunity for a lark. On the spur of the moment, Ike and Edgar decided that it would be great fun to ride down a flooded street using a piece of wooden sidewalk as a raft. With two buddies, they happily floated down Buckeye Street, the main street in town, merrily singing songs like "Marching Through Georgia."

Just as Ike and his crew approached the swollen Mud Creek, a man on horseback yelled at them and demanded that they come ashore. Ike knew that they should obey the stranger, because the water was becoming swift and deep. Fortunately, they did obey. If they had stayed on the raft, the raging water in the flooded creek would have pulled them under, and their adventure would have ended in disaster.

When the boys failed to come home when they were expected, Ike's parents became terribly worried and sent groups of neighbors out searching for them. When Ike and Edgar finally did return, Ida and David were delighted to see them. Because of their foolhardy escapade, however, the boys were sent to bed without any supper.

Along with his fun-loving nature, Ike liked his schoolwork, especially history and mathematics. In high school, he enjoyed plane geometry and became very skilled in the subject. Once, as an experiment, his teacher took away Ike's textbook before an exam to see if he could still pass the course. Ike was delighted when he not only passed the exam, but received an A+.

Although Ike enjoyed math, his favorite subject was history. At one time in high school, he was so fond of Greek and Roman history that he shirked his chores to read books on the subject. Often his mother had to remind him to pitch in with the housework, but he usually ignored her. Once she became so annoyed that she locked his history books in a closet.

Later, his favorite subject became American history. George Washington was his hero, and he read every book he could about the Revolutionary War. He was also fascinated by the Civil War, but when Ike was growing up, there were few books about the Civil War because it had happened comparatively recently. When he had the opportunity, Ike loved to listen to veterans of that war tell stories about their experiences. Most of these men had fought on the Union side, since Kansas had entered the United States as a Free State in 1861.

Throughout his life, Ike enjoyed studying history. He said, "Since those early years, history of all kinds, and certainly political and military, has always intrigued me mightily. . . ."[12]

In their senior year, the brothers' pictures appeared on the same page in the yearbook, with the prediction that Edgar would become president of the United States for two terms, and that Dwight would be a history professor at Yale University.

By the time Ike was ready to graduate, he realized that his first goal in life was to go to college. He had earned good grades in high school, and he knew he needed more education to become a success in whatever career he might choose. He also dreamed of playing on a college football team.

The Eisenhowers had always hoped their sons would go to college, but, unfortunately, could not afford the tuition for six children. Ike had known for a long time that he would have to earn the money for a university education himself.

Ike also understood that to achieve what he wanted in life, he would have to work hard and make sacrifices. Just before he graduated in the spring of 1909, he worried about getting into college. Eventually, he thought of a scheme— a plan that included his brother Edgar.

CHAPTER TWO

"The Class the Stars Fell On"

Ike and Edgar listened to the speaker at their graduation from Abilene High School say, "I would sooner begin life . . . with one arm . . . than attempt to struggle without a college education." [1] Ike took the words to heart. He knew that he must find a way to raise the tuition for his own education.

After talking the matter over, he and Edgar decided to help each other. They concluded that since Edgar was older, he should enroll at the University of Michigan. Ike would work a year at the local creamery, sending Ed part of his earnings to help him meet college expenses.

Ike worked hard at his job, but after a year, he became discouraged. He realized that it would take a long time for him and Ed to graduate from college if they used this plan of only going to college every other year.

During the summer of 1910, Ike and his good friend Everett Hazlett, nicknamed "Swede," saw a lot of each other. Swede had applied to the Naval Academy at Annapolis. Ike thought that the military academies might interest him. After getting Swede's advice on how to apply, Ike wrote a letter to Senator Joseph L. Bristow, Republican from Kansas, requesting an appointment to either Annapolis or West Point.

A few months later, Ike took the competitive entrance examinations for both academies. He was surprised and excited when he came out number one on the Annapolis exam. But, because he had stayed out of college to work, and was now almost twenty-one years old, he was too old to enter Annapolis.

Then Ike heard that he came out second on the West Point examination. After learning that the man who made first place had failed the physical exam, Ike was overjoyed when Senator Bristow gave him an appointment to West Point for the spring of 1911.

Ike realized how lucky he was to be able to receive an expense-paid four-year college education. Now he dreamed of playing on the Army football team.

Unfortunately, his family did not share his enthusiasm. Ida and David, devoutly religious, did not believe in anything to do with the military. Ike's mother was very much opposed to war and was disappointed that her son would be in the army. Trying to hide her displeasure, she told Ike that it was his choice. Later, Ike's younger brother Milton told Ike that after he left on the train for West Point, his mother went up to her room and cried for a long time.

Even Ike's high school math teacher tried to discourage him from going to West Point. She told him, "There's just no future in the army. You're just throwing yourself away."[2]

But in spite of these negative reactions from his family and his teacher, Ike looked forward to going to the military academy. Boarding the train for West Point, he wore his only suit and carried a few clothes in a well-worn suitcase. On the way to New York, Ike stopped in Ann Arbor at the University of Michigan to visit Edgar. The two

*Ike's parents were pacifists and would
not have chosen a military career
for their son. Front row left to right:
David, Milton, and Ida. Back row:
Dwight, Edgar, Earl, Arthur, and Roy.*

brothers had an enjoyable few days together. One night they dated two college girls, and during the evening went canoeing on Lake Huron. Ike said it was the most romantic evening he had ever spent. He began to wonder if perhaps he had made a mistake in not going to the University of Michigan with Ed.

When he arrived at West Point on June 14, 1911, Ike was impressed by the fortress-like buildings and the spectacular view from the palisades overlooking the Hudson River. What a different scene from the plains of Kansas!

He received his uniforms, and an instructor gave the cadets, in Ike's words, "a series of shouts and barks . . . telling us to run here and run there; pick up our clothes; . . . put our shoulders back . . . and to keep running, running, running; . . . everything was on the double."[3]

Exhausted at the end of the day, Ike kept reminding himself that he was getting a free college education.

By evening, all of the new recruits were called together to be sworn in as cadets of the United States Military Academy. Ike wrote: "A feeling came over me that the expression 'The United States of America' would now and henceforth mean something different than it ever had before. From here on it would be the nation I would be serving, not myself. Suddenly the flag itself meant something. . . ."[4]

The first year at West Point proved difficult for many of the cadets. Some of them dropped out because they could not handle the vigorous training and the hazing by the upperclassmen.

Ike's friend and classmate, Omar Bradley, said they were "taught how to make a bed, clean and care for their room; when to shave; when to shine our shoes; and always, always, to say 'sir' to our superiors."[5]

Ike managed to survive the strict training, partly because he was two years older than many of the other cadets and accustomed to hard work. Although he studied enough to pass his exams, Ike managed to get into trouble quite often during his college career. After finishing his studies, he played poker with his buddies and sometimes engaged in pranks. Although his goal was to get a college education, he intended to have a good time while doing so.

During Ike's first year at the Point, he and his friend Tommy Atkins were once told to report to the company corporal in "full dress coats," which meant that they were to be in full uniform wearing their dress coats. Ike and Tommy thought it would be fun to show up with only their "full dress coats" on and nothing else.

In the corporal's room, Ike and Tommy, naked except for their fancy coats, said, "Sir, Cadets Eisenhower and Atkins report as ordered."[6]

Furious, the corporal ordered Ike and Tommy to leave and return properly dressed. For this and other offenses, Ike had to walk punishment tours, which consisted of marching back and forth numerous times on a large field. Ike never avoided punishment by blaming someone else for his misbehavior.

Another time, Ike got into trouble because he danced too exuberantly at a college hop. He did not usually go to cadet dances, but one day he met the attractive daughter of one of his professors and invited her to the party. Ike and his date whirled wildly around the dance floor all evening. The commandant reprimanded him twice for this wild dancing, but Ike paid no attention. The next day, the commandant lost his patience and demoted Eisenhower from cadet sergeant to private.

During his years at West Point, Ike did not take his troubles too seriously. He said, "I enjoyed life at the Academy, had a good time with my pals, and was far from disturbed by an additional demerit or two."[7]

Ike seldom dated at West Point, because he had met a girl in Abilene. Blonde, blue-eyed Gladys Harding was considered the prettiest girl in town. She lived with her family in the wealthier north district, and her father certainly did not approve of her going out with Ike. He told his daughter, "Get rid of that Eisenhower kid. He'll never amount to anything."[8] Her father's attitude, however, did not discourage Ike. He wrote to Gladys often and saw her when he visited Abilene. One Christmas, he even invited her to meet him in New York City during his brief vacation.

After he returned to West Point, he wrote to her, saying, ". . . your love is my whole world. Nothing else counts at all. . . . I love you, girl, and shall never cease. Your devoted Dwight."[9]

Sports were Ike's main interest in college. By his sophomore year, he was a halfback on the Army football team and considered a fast and aggressive player. Before long, he earned his letter and was chosen for the varsity team. He was such a good player that his teammates predicted that he would be picked as an All-American. In one memorable game, he played against Jim Thorpe, the famous Indian player on the Carlisle team, the winner of the decathlon and pentathlon events in the 1912 Olympics. In that game, Army lost to Carlisle—24 to 6.

Ike and Omar Bradley played on the same football team. Both men were devoted to the sport and felt that the game developed strong character.

Bradley later said, "In those days West Point was sports oriented to a feverish degree . . . in organized team sports one learns the important art of group cooperation in goal achievements. No curricular endeavor I know of could better prepare a soldier for the battlefield."[10]

Unfortunately, Ike's football career did not last very long. His dreams were shattered in a game against Tufts

*Although he was at West Point for an education,
Ike considered football just as important, and
he was a very good player.*

College. As he plunged through the line, a tackler grabbed his foot, and Ike twisted to get free. When he couldn't, he severely injured his knee. He was crushed when, because of this injury, the doctor refused to let him play in the game against Navy two weeks later.

After his knee began to heal, Ike had another accident. This time it occurred while he rode horseback. In a drill, he had to leap off his horse and jump over the horse while it took a low hurdle. Sadly, Ike landed on his injured knee and collapsed on the ground. He was hospitalized for four days. There, several doctors told him that he could no longer participate in rugged sports, such as football.

Brokenhearted, Ike considered quitting college. Several times his friends had to talk him out of leaving. He said, "I have often wondered why, at that moment, I did not give increased attention to studies. . . . I gave less. . . . Life seemed to have little meaning."[11]

By the following year, Ike changed his mind and decided to continue at West Point. Although his football days were over, he still loved sports, and he was pleased to be appointed an assistant football coach and a cheerleader.

Ike had another blow just before he graduated from West Point. Colonel Shaw of the medical department recommended that, because of his knee injury, Ike should not be commissioned in the cavalry. The colonel wanted him to enter the coast artillery. Angry and disappointed, Ike refused to accept this alternative.

He decided that if he couldn't get a commission in the army, he would resign and go to South America, perhaps Argentina. Colonel Shaw decided to reconsider, however, if Ike would promise not to go into the cavalry where he would be required to ride horseback. Overjoyed to receive his commission in the army, Ike wrote on his preference card with regard to the type of service he wished, "Infantry—first, Infantry—second, and Infantry—third."[12]

So, after a tumultuous college career, Ike graduated from West Point in the class of 1915, standing 61st in a class of 164 cadets academically, and 125th in conduct.

Ike had enjoyed college, and in spite of the demerits, he knew that he had obtained an excellent education. He was twenty-four years old and had accomplished his first goal: graduating from college. In the process, he had overcome two major disappointments: no longer being able to play football, and not being assigned to the cavalry. Ike knew, however, that he was popular with his classmates, and he hoped he would be a good leader. At the time, Omar Bradley said, "Ike liked people and it is awfully hard for them not to like him in return."[13]

Now ready to graduate, Ike was eager to receive his orders as an army lieutenant. It was the spring of 1915, and World War I had begun in Europe, although the United States was still an observer in that terrible conflict. Ike wondered about his future.

Ike and his West Point graduating class of 1915 later became world famous, for during World War II this class was known as "the class the stars fell on."[14] This graduating class produced fifty-nine generals, including two five-star generals: Eisenhower and Omar Bradley; two four-star generals: James Van Fleet and Joseph McNarney; and seven three-star generals. Over one-third of the class reached the rank of general.

CHAPTER THREE

"That Was the Entrance into My Life of Mamie Geneva Doud"

After graduation from West Point, Ike received his first assignment as a brand-new second lieutenant in the 19th Infantry Regiment at Fort Sam Houston, Texas. This army base was located a few miles north of San Antonio, a pleasant Texas city, which still retained some of its early Spanish culture.

By this time, Ike's romance with Gladys Harding had cooled off. She had either taken her father's advice and agreed that Ike would never amount to anything, or she had decided that she would rather tour the country with a musical group with which she played the piano and sang.

When Ike was assigned to Fort Sam Houston, he did not have a girlfriend and was not especially interested in meeting any women. One day several weeks after he arrived at his new post, Ike began making his rounds of inspection as officer of the day, when he saw a small group of people across the street. Among them was Mrs. Harris, a friendly woman whom Ike had recently met. Later, Ike wrote about this incident.

Mrs. Harris called to him. "Won't you come over here?"

Ike replied, "I have to start an inspection trip."

He later learned that she said to the others, "Humph, the woman hater of the post."

Mrs. Harris continued persuading him, "Just come over here and meet these friends of mine." [1] Ike reluctantly walked over to the group.

Mrs. Harris introduced him to the gathering, which included a young woman wearing a white linen dress and a floppy black hat. Ike said, "The one who attracted my eye instantly was a vivacious and attractive girl, smaller than average, saucy in the look about her face and in her whole attitude. If she had been intrigued by my reputation as a woman hater, I was intrigued by her appearance. . . . That was the entrance into my life of Mamie Geneva Doud." [2]

Impulsively, Ike invited her to make the rounds of the guard posts with him and was surprised when she agreed to accompany him.

Mamie thought at the time that he was the handsomest man she had ever seen.

When they met, Mary Geneva Doud, known as Mamie, was eighteen years old. She lived in Denver, Colorado, but because of the cold climate there, she and her family often spent the winter in San Antonio. Her family was wealthy; her father was an executive in a meat-packing company and a real estate investor. While growing up, Mamie and her two younger sisters had received the advantages of a good education, travel, and many luxuries. Unfortunately, as a young girl, Mamie was often in poor health, which caused her to be absent from school much of the time. Thus, her education suffered.

Mamie was a sociable girl who loved going to parties and wearing fashionable dresses. One classmate called her a "gay, cheery girl who adored pretty clothes." [3] She was also a talented singer and pianist, Gilbert and Sullivan tunes being her favorites.

Since Mamie and her family spent every winter in San Antonio, she had met many young men there who liked to take her to parties and dances. In fact, she was so popular that when she first met Ike, she kept him waiting four weeks for their first date.

When Mamie finally decided to go out with him, Ike was delighted. Soon he fell in love with her, and they began to see each other as often as Ike could get off the base.

Ike loved a good time, and when off duty and not dating Mamie, he enjoyed playing baseball and poker with other officers on the army base. The younger officers had to make their own amusements, since none of them had much spending money.

One evening, Ike and several of his officer friends were standing around near the post flagpole, which was held up by supporting cables. Ike told his friend Lt. Adler that he could overhand his way to the top of the flagpole. The two young men had a five-dollar bet on it. When Ike was nearing the top, a colonel saw him. He yelled to Ike, "Who is that up on that cable?"

Ike shouted down, still holding on to the wire, "Mr. Eisenhower, Sir."

The older man said, "Come down here."

Ike replied, "Sir, Mr. Adler and I have a bet. He put down five dollars that I cannot overhand my way to the top of this cable . . . so could I please go on . . . ?"

Exasperated, the colonel demanded, "Do as I say and do it right now. Get down here!"[4]

Ike reluctantly obeyed. After the colonel left, Lt. Adler claimed that he had won the bet, but Ike insisted that he had. Finally, the onlookers persuaded Ike and Adler to declare the bet a draw.

In spite of such lighthearted recreation, Ike found that life on the base was not all fun and games. He discovered that the people in Texas felt somewhat removed from World War I, because it was being fought in Europe. But they were concerned about the border, where the Mexican bandit Pancho Villa often crossed into the United States and made illegal raids, terrorizing the Texans.

Texas had a history of involvement in disputes with Mexico. In fact, the army base had been named for Sam Houston, the commander of the Texas army that fought for independence from Mexico in 1835.

Because of the trouble with Mexico in 1915, Ike became part of a group of American soldiers sent to patrol the Mexican border. One night, some of Pancho Villa's guerrillas ambushed him and fired several shots in his direction. Fortunately, all of the shots missed. Because of this near-miss, Ike's companions nicknamed him "Lucky Ike."

During his first year on the army base, every time Ike had leave, he called on Mamie. When Ike realized that Mamie loved him too, he decided to propose to her. On Valentine's Day in 1916, he asked her to marry him. After Mamie happily accepted, he gave her an exact duplicate of his West Point class ring as an engagement ring. But, since Mamie was only nineteen, her family thought she was too young to marry. The young couple promised to wait until November, when Mamie would be twenty years old.

As their romance progressed, Ike became very fond of Mamie's entire family. He especially liked talking to her father, John Doud, who was also interested in sports. Before long, Mr. Doud was treating Ike like a son.

Her father warned Mamie that it might be hard for her to get used to living on a second lieutenant's salary, because she had always had all of the spending money she wished. But Mamie was sure that she could manage on Ike's pay.

Just before their marriage, Ike applied for the aviation section of the signal corps. Ike was anxious to learn to fly, and he knew that he would make more money in this branch of the army. (In 1915, the air force did not exist.)

Ike was pleased when he learned that he had been accepted in the aviation branch. He went to the Doud home to announce his exciting news. After making this announcement, Ike said that, "there was some chilliness in the atmosphere; indeed, the news of my good fortune was greeted with a large chunk of silence."[5]

Then Ike was amazed when Mr. Doud said that, ". . . if I were so irresponsible as to want to go into the flying business just when I was thinking of being married, he and Mrs. Doud would have to withdraw their consent."[6] At that time, everybody thought that flying was an exceedingly risky undertaking.

Disappointed at Mr. Doud's decision, Ike realized that Mamie was more important to him than learning to fly, so he told Mr. Doud he would give up aviation and remain in the infantry.

He now resolved that he must develop "a more serious attitude toward life, perhaps I should take a broader look at my future in the military. Possibly I had been too prone to lead a carefree, debt-ridden life. Now I would set my sights on becoming the finest Army officer I could, regardless of the branch in which I might serve."[7]

The year Ike and Mamie became engaged, it looked as if the United States was on the verge of entering World War I. And, since he was a professional soldier, Ike wanted to go to Europe as soon as the United States entered the war. He and Mamie persuaded her parents to advance the date of the wedding.

Just before the wedding, Ike was able to get a ten-day leave. He took the train to Denver, where he and Mamie were married on July 1, 1916, by a Presbyterian minister in the spacious Doud home on Lafayette Street. At the ceremony, Ike knew that Mamie, dressed in her white Chantilly lace dress, was the most beautiful bride he had ever seen. Ike wore his best starched white dress uniform for the event.

One of Mamie's sisters said that Mamie ". . . was very nervous, but nobody who didn't know her would have known it. Most people didn't realize it, but when she wanted to be, Mamie was very self-possessed. The steel in her didn't show, but she had it."[8]

Ike, Mamie, and the Doud family were the only people at the ceremony. Mamie later said that their wedding was the only time she ever saw her husband nervous.

After the ceremony, a champagne reception was held for a few friends. Ike proudly cut the first piece of wedding cake with his sword, a West Point tradition.

Although Ike and Mamie were extremely happy, some of Mamie's friends did not approve of her marriage. One girl later said, "To begin with, everybody thought Mamie was too young to get married. Then, the Douds were well-off financially, and with all the other beaux she had, . . . Mamie could have done a good deal better. After all, he was only a soldier and a poor boy, and everybody felt he was marrying above his class."[9]

If Ike knew of the ill-feeling of some of Mamie's friends, he simply ignored it.

After the wedding, the Doud family's chauffeur drove the young couple to Eldorado Springs, where they spent part of their honeymoon. Later they traveled to Abilene, so that Mamie could meet the Eisenhower family. David and Ida were delighted with their new daughter-in-law, especially since Ike was the first of their sons to marry.

Mamie was excited to meet Ike's family. After being introduced to Earl and Milton, she remarked, "At last I have some brothers."[10]

When the young Eisenhowers returned to their quarters at Fort Sam Houston, they were greeted by friends who presented them with many wedding gifts. As the weeks

Dwight and Mamie were married in 1916.

went by, Ike and Mamie enjoyed entertaining in their small apartment. They had so many parties that their friends called their apartment "Club Eisenhower."

Because of his marriage, Ike tried hard to advance in his career and was pleased to receive his promotion to first lieutenant the day of his wedding.

The couple's happy existence was rudely interrupted, however. On April 6, 1917, the United States declared war on Germany. Many Americans thought World War I would be the last war ever fought, calling it the "war to end all wars."

Ike, like most young army officers, wanted to go overseas and fight with General Pershing's American troops in France. He immediately applied for overseas duty, for he felt that his career depended on being in combat. But his superior officers had other ideas. Since Ike proved to be good at training men, the army sent him to Fort Oglethorpe, in Georgia, to help construct a miniature battlefield and instruct troops in methods of warfare.

In the meantime, Mamie was expecting their first child. When the baby arrived, Ike was on training duty in the mock battlefield in Georgia and did not hear the news for several days. He was overjoyed when he finally learned he had a son, Doud Dwight. The baby was born on September 24, 1917.

The next year, Ike and Mamie and their baby, nicknamed "Icky," were transferred to Fort Meade, in Maryland. Ike, now an officer in the 65th Engineers Tank Battalion, was delighted to have his family with him on the base.

Although Ike still wanted to go overseas and fight the war, he later was transferred to another tank unit at Camp Colt in Gettysburg, Pennsylvania. He and Mamie loved the green rolling countryside around Gettysburg. On weekends, they often visited the National Military Park, a

*Ike was an officer when he was transferred
to a tank unit at Camp Meade, Maryland.*

memorial to the battle that was the turning point of the Civil War. As an army officer, Ike was intrigued by the military strategy used by the generals from both the Union and Confederate armies in the Battle of Gettysburg.

In October, just before his twenty-eighth birthday, Ike finally got his wish. He received orders to go overseas. He was thrilled that at last he would see the war firsthand. His orders were to embark for France on November 18, to command an armored tank unit. Ike put Mamie and little Icky on a train for Denver, and then he proceeded to New York to leave for Europe.

But as luck would have it, he was destined to remain in the United States, because on November 11, 1918, Germany signed the Armistice ending World War I, and Ike's orders were canceled. In his office, he complained to Captain Norman Randolph, "I suppose we'll spend the rest of our lives explaining why we didn't get into this war. . . ."[11]

He said, "During the First World War every one of my frantic efforts to get to the scene of action had been defeated. . . ."[12] Ike would even have been happy to take a reduction in rank to go overseas.

When the war ended, Ike's rank was cut from lieutenant colonel to the permanent rank of captain, and he was put in charge of discharging thousands of men from the army. Later, he spent several months traveling with a truck convoy from the East Coast to San Francisco.

After the war, Ike was discouraged and wanted to resign from the army and pursue another career, because he realized that some of his brothers and friends were advancing in their careers and earning more money than he was. Once he said, "If not depressed, I was mad, disappointed, and resented the fact that life had passed me by."[13]

His outlook, however, improved after he resettled at Camp Meade, Maryland, and Mamie and Icky were able to join him. Ike and Mamie adored their little son. Ike liked to show him off to his army buddies. In fact, little Icky became a mascot for Ike's army unit. The soldiers had a small uniform made for him and occasionally took him along on their drills.

At Camp Meade, Ike's best friend was George Patton, a feisty and enthusiastic army officer. Older than Ike, Patton had graduated from West Point in 1909. During the war he had been an officer in the tank corps in France. Now, Ike and Patton were in the same army unit and shared similar ideas about the future of tank warfare.

During their spare time, Ike and Patton wrote articles for military magazines on the future of tanks in combat, claiming that tanks should play a more prominent part in warfare. They conceived the idea that a large group of tanks should operate independently of the infantry in swift, deep maneuvers. In 1920, this was a new idea, which their superior officers would not accept. Ike and Patton were advised by their superiors to stop publishing such radical articles.

The Eisenhower and Patton families became very friendly during this time, and often attended the same parties. At a dinner in the Pattons' home, Ike met General Fox Conner, who had been General Pershing's right-hand man during the war in Europe. General Conner immediately liked Ike and was interested in the two younger officers' ideas about tank warfare.

Ike and Mamie were happily settled at Camp Meade when a tragedy occurred. They were planning a big Christmas celebration for their little boy, when suddenly he caught scarlet fever from their maid. Because the disease was contagious, the doctor wouldn't let Ike go into the sick boy's room. Ike was terribly upset. A devoted father, he sat on the porch of their home and waved to his son through the window. Sometimes he called to Icky from the doorway.

Tragically, just after New Year's, Icky died. Ike and Mamie were devastated with grief. Ike said, "We were completely crushed. . . . I have never known such a blow."[14] Fifty years later, Ike wrote about the death of Icky, saying it was the greatest disappointment and disaster in his life.

After this tragedy, Ike tried to muster all the courage he could, for he knew that life must go on. Not long after Icky's death, he received an overseas assignment. Perhaps this was the opportunity he needed to get his mind off his grief.

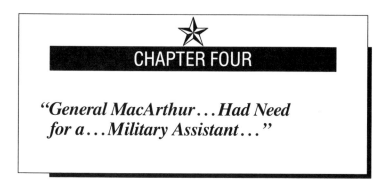

CHAPTER FOUR

"General MacArthur...Had Need for a...Military Assistant..."

In spite of the temptation to pursue another career, Ike decided to remain in the army. Now his goal in life was to become an outstanding officer. His decision was based on two beliefs. First, he knew that the American way of life was worth fighting for, and second, he felt comfortable in the army and enjoyed the chance to travel and meet important people.

During the early years of Ike's army career, there were four exceptional generals who played important roles in his life: Fox Conner, John J. Pershing, Douglas MacArthur, and George C. Marshall. Ike learned a great deal from these men, for each helped him become a competent officer.

Of the four, Brigadier General Fox Conner was probably Ike's favorite superior officer, and the most helpful to him. When General Conner was commanding the 20th Infantry Brigade at Camp Gaillard in the Panama Canal Zone, he requested that Ike be his executive officer. Ike and Mamie traveled to Panama in January 1922.

The Eisenhowers found Panama a complete change from their other tours of duty. Mamie hated the hot and rainy climate. She described their house, which was built on stilts, as "a double-decked shanty, only twice as disreputable."[1] The big black bats that visited their home occasionally terrified her.

The Eisenhowers lived next door to General and Mrs. Conner. After Mamie and Virginia Conner became good friends, Virginia helped Mamie cope with the many inconveniences of living in a tropical country.

The American army was in Panama to defend Culebra Cut, part of the Panama Canal, in the event of hostile action. Ike and General Conner had plenty of time on their visits to various posts to ride horseback and talk, and they soon became good friends.

Because of Fox Conner, Ike renewed his interest in history. The general loaned him books about military campaigns and strategy, and philosophy. Later, Ike said that what he learned from General Conner was equal to a graduate course in military affairs.

During their tour of duty in Panama, Mamie became pregnant with her second child. Since she wanted the baby born in the United States, she sailed by ship to New Orleans and then took a train to Denver to stay with her parents. Just before the baby arrived, Ike took a leave of absence and arrived in Denver shortly before John Sheldon Doud Eisenhower was born on August 3, 1922.

Both Mamie and Ike were delighted with John. The excitement of his birth helped them adjust to the heartbreak of losing their first son. Ike said that John was the image of Icky, and Mamie almost smothered the new baby with love.

Ike and Mamie returned to Panama where they spent three more years. During that time, Ike continued his friendship with General Fox Conner. Conner's favorite words of wisdom to Ike were, "Always take your job seriously, never yourself."[2]

*John, here at two and a half years old
with Mamie, helped Eisenhower recover
from the death of his first son.*

The general gave Ike other good advice. He said that there would certainly be another world war, and that Ike should prepare himself for it. He advised Ike to try to get an assignment under Colonel George C. Marshall, who would undoubtedly have an important position in the next war.

After three years in Panama, Ike, now a major, was sent back to Fort Meade to command a tank battalion and also be the base football coach. A few months after his return, restless and dissatisfied with his new assignment, Ike felt that his career was at a standstill. He requested that he be sent to Infantry School, because he thought this would advance his career. Unfortunately, his request was denied.

At this point, Ike was discouraged and frustrated. Then one day he received a mysterious telegram: "No matter what orders you receive from the War Department make no protest accept them without question Signed Conner."[3]

Ike was puzzled by the telegram, but soon he received orders to go to Colorado for recruiting duty. He knew that this was the worst assignment any army officer could receive. Still he had faith in Conner's advice and went to Colorado.

To his surprise, Ike soon learned that his next assignment was to attend Command and General Staff School at Fort Leavenworth, Kansas. He was overjoyed. "I was ready to fly—and needed no airplane!"[4] Then he realized that General Conner had helped him get this very special duty.

At Fort Leavenworth, Ike knew that he had to work harder than he had ever worked before. His challenge was to compete with 245 men in his class, most of whom had already graduated from the Infantry School which Ike had not attended. He tried not to be discouraged when an aide to the chief of infantry advised him to drop out of this school, because "you will probably fail."[5]

In spite of this prediction, as soon as Ike attended his classes in military strategy and war games, he realized that he had learned so much from General Conner that he could pass the courses without much difficulty. At the end of the year, Ike graduated first in the class of 245.

After graduation, Ike was sent to command a battalion in Fort Benning, Georgia, and then to Washington, D.C., to write a guidebook to the American battlefields of World War I.

In Washington, Ike's immediate superior was the famous General John J. Pershing, who led the American Expeditionary Force in Europe during World War I. General Pershing had been nicknamed "Black Jack," because he was a strict and stern officer. But, in spite of Pershing's dour disposition, Ike liked the general.

Later, General Pershing recommended Ike for the Army War College in Washington, D.C., which was the highest honor any young officer could receive. Ecstatic, Ike wrote, "To graduate from the War College had long been the ambition of almost every officer and I was anxious to take the assignment."[6] After graduating from the War College in June 1928, Ike knew that he had received the very best military education possible. He hoped that some day he could put all his knowledge to good use.

After his graduation, Ike had the choice of two assignments: to stay with the general staff in Washington, or to go to Paris to revise the book on American battlefields. Ike wanted to remain in Washington, but since Mamie was anxious to see Paris, she urged him to take that assignment. Ike didn't object because he had never seen Europe. Thus, partly to please Mamie and partly for his own pleasure, Ike took the European assignment. After arriving in France, Ike truly enjoyed living in Paris.

A few years later, Ike met another general who had a profound effect on his life. In 1930, while on assignment in the office of the assistant secretary of war in Washington, D.C., Ike was closely associated with General Douglas MacArthur, the army chief of staff.

Having graduated first in his class from West Point in 1903, MacArthur was a brilliant though controversial man. He had such a good memory that he could read through a speech and then repeat it word for word.

In Washington, General MacArthur thought that Eisenhower was a competent young officer and wanted Ike to work for him. In 1932, Ike joined the general's staff as a personal military assistant. For the next six years, MacArthur would be Ike's boss, or superior officer.

Ike had mixed feelings about the general, because he often disagreed with MacArthur's policies and thought that the general was egotistical. For example, MacArthur frequently talked of himself in the third person. He would say when speaking of himself, "So MacArthur went over to the senator, and said, 'Senator, . . .' "[7]

MacArthur had the reputation among his colleagues of being dictatorial. One acquaintance said, "If Caesar didn't look like MacArthur, he should have."[8]

But in some ways, Ike admired MacArthur. Ike said, "He did have a hell of an intellect. . . . My God, he was smart. He had a brain. . . ."[9]

At this time, MacArthur thought Ike was an extremely able officer. In a fitness report, he wrote of Ike, "This is the best officer in the Army. When the next war comes, he should go right to the top."[10]

By 1935, the Philippines was in the process of becoming a fully independent country. Roosevelt assigned MacArthur as the military adviser to Philippine President Manuel Quezon to help develop an army for this new nation. Some officials, however, thought that Roosevelt had sent MacArthur to these Pacific islands to get him out of Washington, since the two men often disagreed.

At this time, General MacArthur requested that Ike

be his assistant in the Philippines, because MacArthur knew that he couldn't get along without him. Ike was reluctant to leave the United States, however, because Mamie refused to go to another foreign country until John finished school in Washington.

Ike had no choice but to accept the assignment. After they arrived in the Philippines, Ike and General MacArthur helped President Quezon organize an army. At the same time, Ike supervised the building of a new airfield. Ike had always wanted to learn to fly a plane, and he now had the opportunity to fulfill his wish. During his flight training, he remarked, "Because I was learning to fly at the age of forty-six, my reflexes were slower than those of the younger men."[11] But he passed the course, and after logging 350 hours in the air, he was delighted to receive his pilot's wings.

After being alone in the Philippines for many months, Ike was overjoyed when Mamie and John finally came to join him after John had finished the eighth grade. Unfortunately, Mamie was ill much of the time she lived there, and her memories of the Philippines were unhappy ones.

On the other hand, John thoroughly enjoyed his experience in the islands, where he attended the Bishop Brent School for American children in Baguio, 175 miles from Manila. While on vacation, John accompanied Ike on inspection trips around the islands, and father and son often played tennis together, with John usually winning.

Toward the end of Ike's tour of duty, his relationship with MacArthur became strained. The two men had entirely different personalities, and seldom saw eye to eye on any problem. Ike made friends easily with people everywhere, while MacArthur had a formal and aloof nature. Some of their disagreements were caused by the fact that Eisenhower had a closer relationship with Philippine President Quezon than did MacArthur. Ike had become friends with President Quezon, and often enjoyed playing bridge and poker with him.

Ike said, "Probably no one has had more, tougher fights with a senior than I had with MacArthur. I told him time and again, 'Why in hell don't you fire me? . . . you do things I don't agree with and you know damn well I don't.' "[12] The fact was that the general didn't fire Ike because he truly needed him.

By 1938, Europe was in a state of turmoil, since Nazi Germany was becoming increasingly aggressive. Ike felt isolated in the Philippines and wanted desperately to return to the United States. About this time, Ike received an interesting and tempting offer. Many Jews were trying to flee Nazi Germany because they were being persecuted. Some Jewish friends approached Ike with an offer of a civilian job, at $60,000 a year, to seek havens for Jewish refugees in China and Indonesia.

This proposal tempted Ike because the salary was much higher than the one he was receiving. But if he accepted the offer, he would have to resign from the army. Ike decided that since he had worked so hard at his career, he would stay in the military.

In 1938 and 1939, it was apparent that Europe would soon be engulfed in war. At this time, Ike could hardly wait to return to the United States, but President Quezon wanted him to stay, and offered him an increase in pay from the Philippine government. Ike said, "Mr. President, your offer is flattering. But no amount of money can make me change my mind. My entire life has been given to this one thing, my country and my profession. I want to be there if what I fear is going to come about actually happens."[13] By now it was obvious that World War II would soon begin, and Ike wanted to be part of it.

Although he was offered a raise by
Philippine President Quezon as
encouragement to stay in the Philippines,
Eisenhower reviewed the Philippine
troops in 1939 for the last time.
He was anxious to return to Washington.

On September 1, 1939, after Britain and France declared war on Germany, Ike said to General MacArthur, "General, in my opinion the United States cannot remain out of this war for long. I want to go home as soon as possible. . . ."[14]

Ike also wished to return to the states because of Mamie and John. John had recently graduated from high school and was ready to decide about college. One evening, Ike had a long talk with John, during which he told his son that he had found his army career "wonderfully interesting . . . it had brought me into contact with men of ability, honor, and a sense of high dedication to their country."[15]

John's Uncle Edgar, a successful attorney in Tacoma, Washington, offered to put John through law school and give him a position in his law firm. In spite of this generous offer, John decided that he would rather go to West Point, saying that his father had helped him make up his mind.

Thus in 1939, the Eisenhowers prepared to return to Washington. Ike was anxious to go home. After three often disappointing years in the Philippines, Ike wanted his own command. John was eager to apply to West Point. But looking ahead, Mamie feared that she would soon be spending long months alone while her son and husband were far away.

Having spent his entire life learning to be a capable army officer, Ike could compare his army career with an early football experience. During World War I, he watched the war from the bench, because he had not been sent overseas. Now in World War II, he was sure that he would have the opportunity to play with the team. He could hardly wait to get out there and fight.

★

CHAPTER FIVE

*"The Chief Says for You to Hop a Plane
and Get Up Here Right Away..."*

When Ike returned to the United States from the Philippines, Europe had already plunged into World War II. The war began on September 1, 1939, when Adolf Hitler's troops invaded Poland.

For six years, Hitler and the Nazi Party (National Socialist Workers' Party) had ruled over Germany. As early as 1932, the Nazis won an election to control the legislature, called the Reichstag, and the following year Hitler became chancellor of Germany. Hitler wanted to make Germany the most powerful nation in the world. To do this, he pursued the policies of lebensraum, more territory for Germany to expand; racial purity, which advocated a pure Aryan race and the elimination of the Jewish people; and a new European order, by which Germany would rule the world.

The Nazis governed Germany ruthlessly with the help of the secret police, or gestapo, which terrorized Jews and other people who opposed their form of government. The gestapo often seized its victims in the middle of the night, throwing them in jail or prison camps, even shooting them in their shops or homes.

Hitler's power spread rapidly, and by 1939, German troops began seizing neighboring countries by surprise attacks, called blitzkriegs, or lightning wars. In March 1939, German troops seized Czechoslovakia, where they met little resistance. Then on September 1, they marched into Poland. The sudden seizure of Poland proved the turning point for Great Britain and France. These two countries immediately declared war on Germany.

Within the next few days, the Commonwealth countries of Canada, Australia, New Zealand, and South Africa entered the war on the side of Great Britain and France.

Halfway around the world, President Roosevelt announced that the United States would not take sides in the war. But shortly thereafter, the first peacetime draft of young men into the armed services began, indicating that the United States would be prepared for war if it became unavoidable.

Ike, Mamie, and John boarded an ocean liner in December for the states. They spent a happy Christmas together in Hawaii, and arrived in San Francisco to celebrate the new year. During this time, Ike had a premonition that he would play an important role in the army if the United States should enter the war.

After Ike's many years of military training, he now wanted to be in the field training soldiers. He was, therefore, pleased to receive orders to go to Fort Lewis, Washington, to instruct new recruits. He wrote to his friend Omar Bradley about his new job. "I'm having the time of my life. Like everyone else in the army, we're up to our necks in work and in problems, big and little. But this work is fun! . . . I could not conceive of a better job." [1]

Ike didn't even mind the hardships and discomfort of field maneuvers. He said that he froze at night, never had enough sleep, and was often tired. But he enjoyed the experience, for he spent his happiest hours while leading troops.

In the meantime, John had come out first in the competitive exam for West Point. Delighted, Ike said, "This accomplishment of John's has added two inches to my chest and volumes to Mamie's daily conversation about 'her son.' "[2]

After two years of training troops, in September 1941, Ike, now a colonel, was sent to Louisiana. There, in preparation for a real war, two United States armies of 400,000 troops engaged in war games.

In this mock war, as chief of staff of General Krueger's Third Army, Ike planned the strategy for the maneuvers. He must stop the enemy Second Army, which had more armored striking force, from winning the war. At the end of the exercise, the Third Army won the battle, and Ike got the credit.

Ike became famous almost overnight. Drew Pearson, a well-known columnist, described him as having ". . . a steel-trap mind plus unusual physical vigor . . ."[3] Because Eisenhower performed so well in these war games, General Krueger recommended that Ike be promoted to brigadier general. After this promotion, Ike was congratulated by his fellow officers and by the press.

He said, "When they get clear down to my place on the list, they are passing out stars with considerable abandon."[4] Ike never let a promotion go to his head.

In Europe, the Germans had already conquered Holland, Belgium, Luxembourg, and most of France by early summer 1940. At this time, the British were fighting desperately to hold out against the Nazis, who were bombing London daily and had also invaded the Soviet Union in June 1941. In spite of the disastrous Nazi bombings, the English people remained brave, partly because of the example set by Prime Minister Winston Churchill.

In a speech to the House of Commons just after he became prime minister, Churchill said, "I have nothing to offer but blood, toil, tears and sweat." He continued, "The

British must . . . wage war, by sea, land and air with all our might and with all the strength that God can give us." He said their aim was "Victory—victory at all costs, victory in spite of all terror, victory, however long and hard the road may be."5

Influenced by the courage of Churchill, and of the king and queen, who remained in London during the bombings, the British people continued to hold out against the Nazis.

On the other side of the world, Japan had invaded China back in 1937. During the following years, the Japanese tried to acquire more territory in East Asia as rapidly as they could. But the United States paid slight attention to the Japanese until they were forced to in 1941.

On Sunday, December 7, 1941, while stationed at Fort Sam Houston, Texas, Ike went to his office early to catch up on some work. Returning home about noon, he told Mamie that he wanted to rest because he was "dead tired," and that he didn't wish to be "bothered by anyone wanting to play bridge."6

Early that afternoon, Tex Lee, Ike's executive officer, called to tell him of the devastating Japanese attack on Pearl Harbor in Hawaii. In that brutal surprise attack, thousands of Americans died, and several U.S. battleships were sunk. A few days later, Japan struck the Philippines, Guam, Wake, and Hong Kong.

When Ike heard the news of this attack, he was stunned. The next day, the United States declared war on Japan. Germany and Italy then declared war on the United States on December 11. President Roosevelt said that December 7 was a "day that would live in infamy."

After the attack on Pearl Harbor, most Americans were terrified. If the Japanese could attack Pearl Harbor with absolutely no warning, there was a very good chance that they would soon attack the mainland. Americans feared that Japan's next target would be Los Angeles, San Francisco, or Seattle.

Immediately everyone in the country became fully aware that the United States was at war. Every citizen wanted to do everything possible to defeat the enemy. Thousands of young men and many women enlisted in the army, navy, and marines. Suddenly, the country became united in an unprecedented war effort.

Five days after Pearl Harbor, Ike received a call from Colonel Walter Bedell Smith, secretary of the general staff in the War Department in Washington, D.C. "The Chief [General George Marshall] says for you to hop a plane and get up here right away. . . . Tell your boss that formal orders will come through later."[7] Ike was delighted. This phone call meant that he would have an important job in the war.

Ike had always admired General Marshall, who at the time of Pearl Harbor, held the position of army chief of staff. Marshall was ten years older than Ike, a graduate of the Virginia Military Institute, and an extremely capable officer. Ike said of Marshall, "Of Americans I have known personally, I think that George Marshall possessed more of the qualities of greatness than has any other."[8]

When Ike called on Marshall in his Washington office, the general outlined the United States military and naval positions in the Pacific, telling Ike that the evidence seemed to indicate that the Japanese would take the Philippines. He asked Ike what the general line of action should be.

Ike said, "I thought a second and, hoping I was showing a poker face, answered, 'Give me a few hours.' "

Marshall agreed and then dismissed Ike.

After mulling over the problem for an hour or more, Ike returned to General Marshall, saying that he realized the United States had to save the air lifeline through Australia, New Zealand, Fiji, and Hawaii.

He thought it would be difficult to save the Philippine Islands, but that the United States must do everything possible to keep them free.

He told Marshall, "Our base must be Australia, and we must start at once to expand it and to secure our communications to it. In this last we dare not fail. We must take great risks and spend any amount of money required."

The general replied, "I agree with you. . . . Do your best to save them."[9]

Unfortunately, it was too late to save the Philippines. Japan conquered the Philippines in the battles of Bataan and Corregidor.

After Japan seized the Philippines, Ike said that George Marshall ". . . never seemed to doubt that we could win, even when the Philippines had fallen."[10]

On the European battlefront, Great Britain and the Soviet Union were trying desperately to hold out against increasingly aggressive Nazi Germany and Fascist Italy.

The situation in January 1942 looked dim for the Allies (the United States, Britain, the Commonwealth countries, and the Soviet Union). For the United States to meet the demands of waging war in both Europe and the Pacific, General Marshall decided to reorganize the War Department. Marshall needed someone to plan war strategy. He appointed Ike as head of the newly created Operation Division of the War Department. At first Ike was unhappy with his new assignment, because he wanted to be in the field commanding troops and not stuck behind a desk in Washington.

Before long, however, he realized that he had the biggest challenge of his career, the staggering job of planning the Allied invasion of Europe. With other officers, he proposed that the Allies invade France by crossing the English Channel.

At the beginning of the war, France had been an ally of Great Britain. But in 1940, the French government agreed to cooperate with the Nazis when they realized that the Nazis were ready to conquer their country. The pro-Nazi French government was called the Vichy government, since its headquarters were in the town of Vichy. Some of the French, however, remained loyal to the Allies. The Free French, as they were called, were led by General Charles de Gaulle, who had fled to London.

General Marshall approved of Ike's plans to invade France, and later obtained the approval of President Roosevelt. Marshall then flew to London to meet with British officials.

In April, with British approval of the plans to strike the Continent, General Marshall appointed Eisenhower commander in charge of all American troops in Europe. Surprised and pleased with this development, Ike looked forward to going to England. On his flight to London, he hoped and prayed that his many years of military experience had prepared him for his new responsibilities.

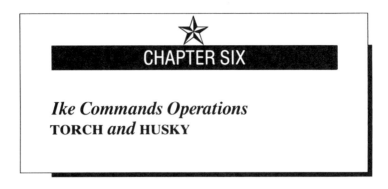

CHAPTER SIX

Ike Commands Operations
TORCH *and* HUSKY

When Eisenhower arrived in London, he saw the terrible destruction the German bombs had caused during the Battle of Britain—demolished buildings, thousands of casualties, and maimed people. He developed an increased hatred for Hitler and the Nazis. Eisenhower knew that this war was no longer a game of strategy, but a life-and-death fight to the finish.

In London he learned that many British leaders, including Prime Minister Churchill, were opposed to the strategy of a 1942 invasion. They felt that the Allies must first regain control of the Mediterranean Sea, at that time dominated by Germany and Italy. The British and Americans decided to first attack North Africa, hoping to free the Mediterranean for Allied shipping.

The combined chiefs of staff (American and British) appointed Eisenhower commander of the entire Allied invasion of North Africa, which was given the code name TORCH. Eisenhower appointed American general Mark Clark as his deputy for the job of planning Operation TORCH. Ike and other top officials knew that TORCH would only postpone the eventual invasion of France.

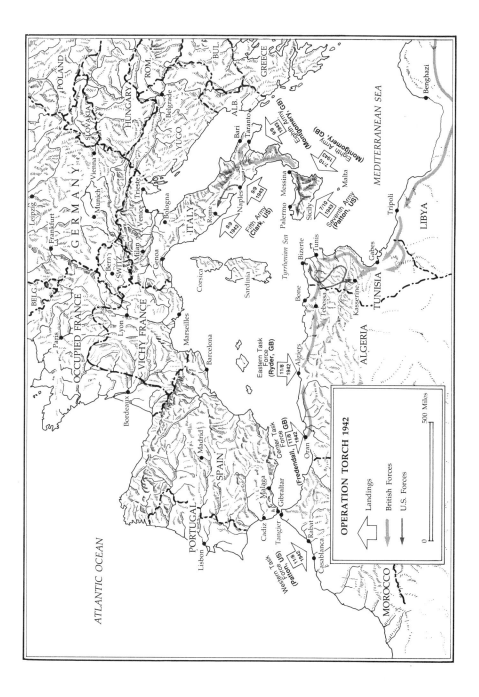

ATLANTIC OCEAN

POLAND

BUL.

GREECE

MEDITERRANEAN SEA

Benghazi

BELG.

OCCUPIED FRANCE

GERMANY

SLOVAKIA

HUNGARY

ROM.

YUGO.

Belgrade

ALB.

Leipzig
Frankfurt
Munich
Vienna

Bern
SWITZ.
Milan
Venice
Trieste
Genoa

Bologna

ITALY

Rome

Bari
Taranto

Naples

Palermo
Messina

Sicily

Malta

Tripoli

LIBYA

Paris
Lyon

VICHY FRANCE

Marseilles

Bordeaux

Corsica

Sardinia

Tyrrhenian Sea

Tunis
Bizerte

Bone

Tebessa

Kasserine

Gabes

TUNISIA

Eighth Army (GB)
(Montgomery, GB)

Eighth Army
(Montgomery, GB)

8/9
1943

7/10
1943

9/9
1943

Seventh Army
(Patton, US)

7/10
1943

9/9
1943

Fifth Army
(Clark, US)

ALGERIA

Barcelona

SPAIN

Madrid

Málaga
Gibraltar

Cádiz
Tangier

PORTUGAL

Lisbon

Rabat

Casablanca

MOROCCO

Eastern Task
Force
(Ryder, GB)

11/8
1942

Center Task
Force
(Fredendall, GB)

11/8
1942

Algiers

Oran

Western Task
Force (US)
(Patton, US)

11/8
1942

OPERATION TORCH 1942

Landings

British Forces

U.S. Forces

0   500 Miles

During the war, Ike was responsible to, and had to comply with, the directives and orders of President Roosevelt, General Marshall, and Prime Minister Churchill and the combined chiefs of staff. In addition, he had to take into consideration the opinions of other American and British generals in his field of operation.

Now Ike had the difficult job of coordinating his plans for Operation TORCH with the British army commanders. He was appointed to this high office instead of a number of other generals because of his popularity in Britain as well as in the United States. Everybody liked General Ike.

In November, Ike moved his headquarters to Gibraltar at the narrow entrance to the Mediterranean Sea from the Atlantic Ocean. The only available office space was an underground cavern beneath the great Rock of Gibraltar, where the Allies set up the signal equipment to keep in touch with the assaulting forces.

Ike and his staff were constantly in touch with hundreds of Allied ships steaming across the North Atlantic toward the northwest coast of Africa. To attack the cities of Algiers and Oran, these ships would pass through the narrow Strait of Gibraltar, where they could easily be attacked by Nazi planes.

Another reason Ike had been chosen to lead TORCH was that the French distrusted the British, since the British had shelled the French fleet in Oran Harbor in 1940. At this time, most of France and North Africa were controlled by the pro-Nazi Vichy French government. The Free French were in exile in various places, some in England, and some in North Africa. Because of the French dislike of the British, the Allied commanders felt that the Americans would get a better reception in North Africa than the British. So the first assaults were made by American troops.

The American troops were led by Ike's old friend

General George Patton. Ike liked Patton, although he was aware of Patton's often egotistical personality. Ike described Patton as "a shrewd soldier who believes in showmanship to such an extent that he is almost flamboyant. . . . He has done well as a combat corps commander. . . ."[1]

Patton met strong resistance at Oran and Casablanca, but within several days, the Americans took the entire area west of Algiers.

In October, after the American troops took the towns of Casablanca, Oran, and Algiers, Ike decided that it was time for the Americans to join the British, under the leadership of Generals Sir Harold Alexander and Sir Bernard Montgomery.

General Montgomery, often called Monty, played a very important role in the war, but he was a man with whom Ike did not always see eye to eye. Ike described Monty as ". . . a very able dynamic type of army commander. . . . He loves the limelight but in seeking it, it is possible that he does so only because of the effect upon his own soldiers, who are certainly devoted to him. . . ."[2]

The British, fighting in El Alamein in Egypt, were pushing German General Erwin Rommel's Afrika Korps troops to the west. At the same time, Ike and General Patton were pushing eastward toward Tunisia. The Allies' aim was to squeeze the German and Italian forces in a nutcracker-type operation in Tunis. The Americans on the west and the British on the east were the nutcracker, the Germans were the nut in the middle.

During this time, Ike spent some of the worst days he had ever experienced. His goal was to take the city of Tunis, which he knew the Allies must gain if they were to control North Africa. He knew that this would be difficult, because the American army did not have enough supplies. To make matters worse, by November and December the weather was so bad that the American troops bogged down. Because the war was going badly, Ike made a personal trip to the front near Tunis to understand the situation. Unfortunately, torrential rains descended over the whole area, and Ike decided that the troops would have to wait until spring to take the town.

On Christmas Eve, Ike received word that French Admiral Darlan, a pro-Vichy Frenchman who was helping the Allies at that time, had been assassinated in Algiers. Ike made a thirty-hour nonstop drive back to his Algerian headquarters. After the trip, he was exhausted, and came down with a severe case of the flu, which caused him to stay in bed for four days.

The bitter battle for Tunisia raged through the winter and spring of 1943, with the Americans fighting from the west and the British from the east. The Allied forces finally converged at Tunis in April, thus defeating the Axis forces (the Germans and Italians).

Although elated with the Allied success, Ike was disappointed to learn that the famous Nazi General Erwin Rommel, nicknamed the "Desert Fox," had escaped before the final battle and returned to Germany.

After the victory in North Africa, Ike knew that the Allies' fortunes were changing. At long last, the Nazis were beginning to retreat to Europe. They were also losing ground on their eastern front, since the Soviet Union had recently defeated the Germans at the Battle of Stalingrad.

Ike's hatred for the Nazis had increased during the past year. He knew the Allies had to defeat the Germans completely if there was ever to be world peace. He wrote, ". . . there grew within me the conviction that as never before in a war between many nations the forces that stood for human good and men's rights were this time confronted by a completely evil conspiracy. . . . Because only by the utter destruction of the Axis was a decent world possible, the war became for me a crusade. . . ."[3]

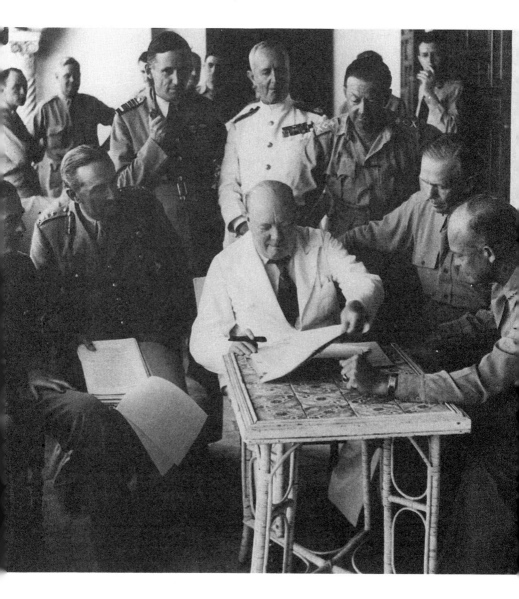

*In Algiers in 1943 the Allies planned
their operations. Seated at the table are
British Prime Minister Winston Churchill,
General Marshall, and General Eisenhower.*

After his success in North Africa, Ike became world famous. Mamie was very proud of him, but with Ike in Europe, and John at West Point, she often felt extremely lonely.

In one of his letters to Mamie, Ike wrote: "Your letters often give me some hint of your loneliness, your bewilderment and your worries in carrying on. . . . So when you're lonely, try to remember that I'd rather be by your side than anywhere else in the world."4 Undoubtedly, the war, and being apart, put a strain on their marriage.

Another possible cause of friction between Mamie and Ike at this time, and later during the war, was that Ike's driver and secretary was an attractive young woman from Ireland, WAC Lieutenant Kay Summersby. Since she and General Ike were often seen together, rumors were spread that they were romantically involved. However, during the early part of the war, she was engaged to an American army officer, who was later killed. The rumors were probably wartime gossip.

After the Allied victory in North Africa, President Roosevelt and Prime Minister Churchill met at Casablanca to make plans for the future. They decided that the next steps would be to capture the island of Sicily, and then to take Italy. The Sicilian campaign was given the code name HUSKY.

After his success in North Africa, Ike was appointed to command Operation HUSKY. In his headquarters in Algiers, Ike met with some of the top-ranking American and British officials to plan the new campaign. Among those present were Prime Minister Churchill, British Foreign Minister Anthony Eden, British Generals Alexander and Montgomery, and United States General Marshall.

In Operation HUSKY, American General Patton and British General Montgomery drove two enemy divisions off Sicily within thirty-eight days.

Next Ike planned to invade Italy, which was a much

more difficult task than the invasion of Sicily. Because of the Vatican and the priceless historical sites in Rome, the Allies had to be careful not to bomb these areas.

After the first cautious Allied bombing raid on Rome on July 24, the Italian dictator, Mussolini, was arrested. King Victor Emmanuel II appointed Marshal Pietro Badoglio as head of a new government.

Since the Allies were short of troops, with most of their forces in England preparing to invade France, Eisenhower's goal was to quickly capture southern Italy. He tried to persuade General Badoglio to make a peace settlement at once, and then change sides and help the Allies.

Ike, however, became frustrated when he received orders from President Roosevelt that the Italians must surrender "unconditionally." This might take a long time. Another reason Ike wanted a quick surrender in southern Italy was that the Germans were rushing additional troops into northern Italy. Eisenhower hoped to negotiate with Badoglio promptly before the Allies lost the entire country.

At his headquarters in North Africa, Ike heard that the Allies successfully entered Italy from four different areas. At this point, he felt greatly encouraged and sent General Walter Bedell Smith, his chief of staff, to Rome to discuss a surrender with General Badoglio. After much bargaining on both sides, Eisenhower planned to announce the surrender agreement on September 9. But in the meantime, he received word that because of German reinforcements in Rome, Badoglio decided not to cooperate.

Ike wanted to settle the war in Italy soon, in order to send Allied troops to England for the invasion of France. He sent a message to General Badoglio saying, "I intend to broadcast the existence of the armistice [an end to the fighting] at the hour originally planned. . . . If you . . . fail to cooperate as previously agreed I will publish to the world the full record of this affair. . . . Failure now on your part to carry out the full obligations to the signed agreement will have the most serious consequences for your country. . . ."[5]

After this announcement, Ike decided to cancel any further air raids on Rome, and prayed that General Badoglio would accept the cease-fire.

As scheduled at six-thirty P.M. on September 9, Ike announced the armistice on the radio in North Africa. "This is General Dwight David Eisenhower, Commander in Chief of the Allied forces. The Italian government has surrendered its armed forces unconditionally. As Allied commander in chief, I have granted a military armistice."[6]

Gambling that the Italians would surrender, Ike waited impatiently for an hour, wondering if General Badoglio would make a similar announcement. Finally, exactly an hour later, the Italian general made the same announcement in Rome. Eisenhower had taken a chance and had bluffed a little. He later said he had "played a little poker . . . and he had won."[7]

After the surrender, many Italians promised to switch sides and help the Allies fight the Germans. Nevertheless, there were many long and difficult battles ahead before the Allies took northern Italy.

With the Allied victory in southern Italy, Ike's fame continued to spread throughout the entire world. His war strategy and forceful personality had made him successful. But Ike knew that sometimes he had to take high risks in order to win.

In December 1943, President Roosevelt met Prime Minister Churchill in Cairo, Egypt, at a summit conference. They decided that it was finally time to cross the English Channel, invade France, and then march on to Germany. This major campaign of the war was called Operation OVERLORD. Ike wondered which general would be chosen to command this all-important battle.

CHAPTER SEVEN

"Okay. We'll Go."

Early in December 1943, President Roosevelt arrived in Tunis, North Africa, on his return from Egypt. When Ike met the president, the first thing Mr. Roosevelt said was, "Well, Ike, you are going to command OVERLORD."[1]

The huge task of invading France and overpowering Nazi Germany now lay ahead. Ike knew that the general who commanded OVERLORD would surely go down in history as the hero of World War II. Eisenhower was really surprised because he had thought the president would appoint General George Marshall, the designer of OVERLORD. But Ike really wanted the assignment and when he got the news, he was flattered and happy. He would have an incredibly important position, supreme commander of all the Allied forces in Europe.

Soon after Eisenhower arrived at his office in London, he received the following order from the combined chiefs of staff: "You will enter the continent of Europe and, in conjunction with the other Allied Nations, undertake operations aimed at the heart of Germany and the destruction of her Armed Forces."[2]

Now confronted with the greatest challenge of his life, Ike realized that if the invasion was to be successful, it would have to be the largest amphibious operation ever undertaken. Together with the British and American high command, he had to plan OVERLORD to the last detail.

The problems were formidable. Above all, both the place and the time of the invasion had to be kept a secret from the Germans. Ike wondered how that would be possible with more than two million men involved.

He knew that the final decisions on all the plans were his alone. Faced with a myriad of problems and complications, Eisenhower realized that OVERLORD could be either a huge success or a disastrous failure. Ike had to use all the knowledge he had acquired during his long army career.

Naturally, Eisenhower was not alone in planning and carrying out Operation OVERLORD. He handpicked many of his subordinates at the Supreme Headquarters, Allied Expeditionary Force (SHAEF). These men were all top-ranking American and British generals and admirals.

One of Ike's main difficulties was getting the full cooperation of each branch of the army, navy, and air force. For instance, when Ike first took over, the combined British and American air forces wanted to act independently. Instead of cooperating with Ike, they decided to bomb targets inside Germany. Ike disagreed. He and Air Marshal Tedder felt that the air force should bomb targets in France, thus making it easier for the Allied invasion.

Ike was adamant on this point, and threatened to resign if he did not have the cooperation of the air force. He knew that unless he had the full cooperation of all the Allied forces, he could not carry on his job as supreme commander. Finally, because of his insistence, the air force did as Ike advised. After the air force bombed railroad lines and bridges near Normandy, the way was prepared for D-Day, the code name for the day set for the invasion of France.

*General Eisenhower planned every
detail of Operation OVERLORD for
all branches of the Allied forces.*

In preparation for D-Day, the southern part of England had become one vast army camp and airfield. Because of possible spies, the British government had stopped all traffic between southern England and the rest of the United Kingdom, including Scotland and Ireland. To fool the enemy, large buildings constructed to house the troops and their supplies were camouflaged so that their purpose could not be guessed if seen from enemy aircraft.

Before D-Day, Eisenhower and the Allies went to great lengths to deceive the Nazis into thinking that the invasion would be at Pas de Calais, a French department (county) directly across the English Channel. Actually, OVERLORD was planned to strike about two hundred miles farther to the southwest on the beaches of Normandy. These beaches were given the code names of Utah and Omaha for the Americans, and June, Gold, and Sword for the British. During the actual invasion, each beach had a different color designation, prominently displayed by an advance scout on the beach, so that each unit would know where it should land.

Ike knew that the troops would need huge amounts of supplies, especially food and ammunition. The artificial harbors for the supply ships were built in advance in England. There were two types: one, called "Mulberries," were complete harbors to be towed to France in pieces; the other, named "Gooseberries," were a line of sunken ships placed stem to stern.

Eisenhower and his staff planned OVERLORD in great detail. First, paratroopers would land behind the enemy lines to prepare the way for the land troops. Then, the amphibious (both land and sea) troops would land on the Normandy beaches, followed by the artificial harbors and troop and supply ships.

After landing, one Allied army group would go to the left and capture the ports of Le Havre and Calais. They

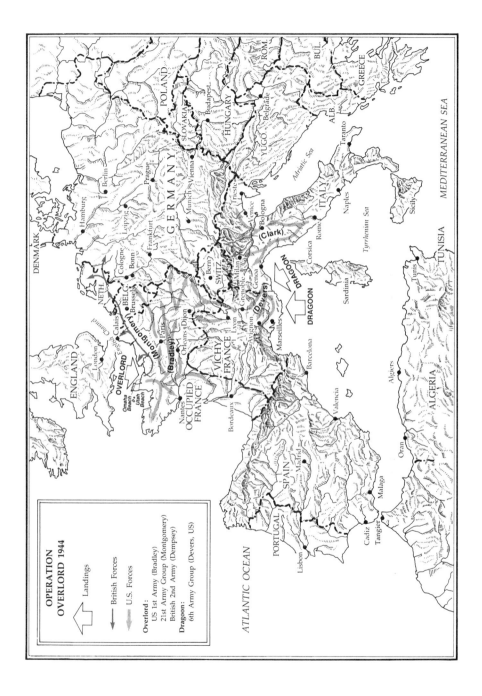

**OPERATION
OVERLORD 1944**

Landings

British Forces

U.S. Forces

Overlord:
US 1st Army (Bradley)
21st Army Group (Montgomery)
British 2nd Army (Dempsey)

Dragoon:
6th Army Group (Devers, US)

ATLANTIC OCEAN

PORTUGAL
Lisbon

SPAIN
Madrid
Barcelona
Valencia
Malaga
Cadiz
Tangier

ENGLAND
London

DENMARK

NETH.
BELG.
Brussels

OCCUPIED
FRANCE
Nantes
Bordeaux

OVERLORD
Omaha Beach
Utah Beach

(Montgomery)
(Bradley)

English Channel
Calais

Paris
Orléans
Dijon

VICHY
FRANCE

Lyon
Grenoble
Avignon
Marseilles

(Devers)
DRAGOON
DRAGOON

SWITZ.
Bern
Milan
Genoa
Turin

GERMANY
Hamburg
Berlin
Leipzig
Cologne
Bonn
Frankfurt
Prague

Munich
Vienna

POLAND

SLOVAKIA

HUNGARY
Budapest

YUGO.
Belgrade

ROM.

BUL.

GREECE

ALB.

ITALY
Corsica
Bologna
(Clark)
Rome
Naples
Sardinia
Taranto

Sicily

ALGERIA
Algiers
Oran

TUNISIA
Tunis

Adriatic Sea

Tyrrhenian Sea

MEDITERRANEAN SEA

Eisenhower talks to paratroopers
in Newbury, England, as they get ready
to load for the D-Day invasion.

would later march to the German border and take the vital Ruhr industrial area. The second army group would go right to join forces with the Allied troops invading southern France.

At the Teheran summit conference, Roosevelt and Churchill had promised Joseph Stalin, the Soviet head of state, that OVERLORD would take place around the first of May 1944. But after Ike began planning, he decided he needed more time to enlarge his forces. D-Day was postponed until June.

For the invasion, the moon, tide, and weather had to be just right. Ike knew that the moon and tide would cooperate on June 5, 6, and 7, but the weather was always uncertain.

Ike stated, "We wanted to cross the Channel with our convoys at night so that darkness would conceal the strength and direction of our several attacks. We wanted a moon for our airborne assaults. We needed approximately forty minutes of daylight preceding the ground assault to complete our bombing and preparatory bombardment. We had to attack on a relatively low tide because of beach obstacles which had to be removed while uncovered . . . the selection of the actual day would depend upon weather forecasts."[3]

During the last weeks before the invasion, Ike spent every spare moment visiting the troops all over England and Scotland. He talked personally to as many men as he could, impressing upon them that Hitler and the Nazis posed a direct threat to their personal freedom. The men appreciated these visits, because they knew that they might die in the attack, and they wanted to feel that their commanders realized their danger.

Before the invasion, Ike had many conferences with "the Prime," as he called Churchill. These were usually held at Chequers, Churchill's country estate, with other

General Eisenhower inspects fliers
after christening the newest
B-17 bomber, the "General Ike."

officials present, often including Foreign Minister Anthony Eden. Most evenings the guests had dinner, viewed a short movie, and then began working about 10:30 P.M. Sometimes they discussed war plans until 3:00 A.M.

On May 15, a final conference of all the Allied generals and admirals and top officials was held at St. Paul's School in London. King George was also present. Both the king and the prime minister spoke. At the end of the conference, Churchill, who had not been enthusiastic about the invasion, said, "Gentlemen, I am hardening toward this enterprise."[4] In other words, he was beginning to approve of OVERLORD.

Ike's headquarters were in Portsmouth, a southern English port town, which would be the embarkation point for the invasion. Ike had now determined that the weather would be right for D-Day on June 5, 6, and 7. But on May 30, Air Chief Marshal Leigh-Mallory predicted a 50 to 70 percent loss of paratroopers and wanted their mission called off.

Ike knew that if he canceled the air strike, he would have to either cancel the landing on the beaches or expect a disastrous beating. Again, Ike, as supreme commander, had to demand the cooperation of the entire Allied Forces. So he called Leigh-Mallory and ordered him to make the air attack as planned.

In addition to all of his concerns, Ike had difficult problems with high officials just before D-Day. Prime Minister Churchill told Eisenhower that he intended to be on one of the invasion ships. Ike realized that he had no power to stop "the Prime," but he was extremely worried about his safety. When King George learned what Churchill planned to do, he was determined to sail on an invasion ship too. Ike was appalled. What would happen if both the British leaders were wounded or killed? Fortunately when Churchill heard of the king's plans, he decided to stay in England and urged the king to do the same.

General Charles de Gaulle, leader of the Free French movement, told the Allies that he wanted to broadcast to the French people as soon as the Allies landed on the Normandy beaches, so that there would be no uprising. President Roosevelt had opposed this idea, so Ike had to compromise with de Gaulle by deciding that on D-Day, both he and the French leader would broadcast to the French citizens.

When June 4 arrived, the day before D-Day, the wind was blowing gale force. Disappointed at this development, Ike knew that he had to postpone the invasion until June 6.

Finally, the night before D-Day, Eisenhower was so worried that he wrote the following message and put it in his pocket, just in case D-Day was a failure. "Our landings in the Cherbourg-Havre area have failed to gain a satisfactory foothold and I have withdrawn the troops. My decision to attack at this time and place was based on the best information available. The troops, the air force and the Navy did all that bravery and devotion to duty could do. If any blame or fault attaches to the attempt, it is mine alone."[5]

On June 5, after hearing a report from his weathermen that the main storm had passed, Ike knew the decision for the invasion was entirely up to him. He alone had to decide if they would strike the next day, June 6. That morning in his Portsmouth office, all the generals and admirals looked at Eisenhower in hushed silence and waited. Ike realized that he had planned OVERLORD the very best he could and he felt confident. Facing the "high brass," he took a deep breath and said, "Okay. We'll go."[6]

These few words set off the largest amphibious force ever gathered.

Shortly after midnight on June 6, 1944, the paratroopers landed near the little town of Sainte Mère Eglise, for the purpose of blocking all the roads so the Germans could not get through. Ike later said, "Now of course they [the paratroopers] got scattered around and that was quite lucky for us. At the time, we thought it was a disaster but because they were scattered so badly, the Germans didn't know anything we were doing . . . they just thought we were crazy."[7]

Next, under cover of darkness, came the naval ships and the landing troops. There were battleships, cruisers, 122 destroyers, 360 motor torpedo boats, and about 6,000 other ships. All of these were able to cross the English Channel undetected by the enemy in the dark of night. Fortunately, because of the continuing bad weather, the Nazi reconnaissance planes had stayed on the ground.

After the first attack, reports came in to Eisenhower, who was still in Portsmouth, from the 101st Airborne units, which he had visited shortly before their takeoff. The reports were that the landings at Utah beach were coming along well, but that there was fierce fighting at Omaha beach. The next day, Ike decided to board a destroyer and visit Omaha beach. When he arrived, he was happy to learn that the Americans had beaten the enemy on the beach and were proceeding inland.

At Omaha beach, Eisenhower conferred with General Bradley. During the rest of the day, he toured all the other beachheads and had a chance to meet with the top commanders, including British General Montgomery. Ike was pleased that the invasion was progressing well.

The battle to gain the beachheads was difficult, and the losses were heavy, but not as bad as Ike had feared. Operation OVERLORD set the stage for the liberation of France and Belgium, the final thrust into Germany, and the eventual Allied victory in the war.

Several events, which Ike didn't know about until much later, probably helped the Allies. Two of Hitler's generals, Field Marshal Erwin Rommel and Field Marshal Gerd von Rundstedt, disagreed on how to fight the Allies.

On one of the French beaches, Eisenhower leans over the side of an amphibious DUCK to consult with one of his unit commanders.

Rommel wanted to crush the Allied troops on the beaches, and von Rundstedt wanted to wait until the troops arrived inland. By D-Day, Hitler had not resolved this argument.

Ironically, Hitler was asleep when the attack first began, and his aide refused to awaken him. Thus, he did not call up the First Panzer Corps to defend the Normandy coast.

Indeed, this failure probably sealed the Nazis' defeat. D-Day went better for the Allies than Ike actually expected. Fortunately, he never had to deliver the message of failure that he had written the night before. The note remained in his pocket. Although at times it had been extremely difficult, Ike was able to persuade all the Allied forces to cooperate and work together as a gigantic team in the largest amphibious landing ever undertaken. He was pleased with the success of OVERLORD, but he knew that this was only a beginning in the eventual defeat of Nazi Germany. He wondered if the next assault on the Nazis would be as successful as OVERLORD, or would the Allies meet with overpowering resistance?

CHAPTER EIGHT

The Americans Say, "Nuts"

Ike was relieved after the success of D-Day, happy that the Allies were finally seriously challenging the Nazis on several fronts. But he realized that the Normandy landing was only the beginning of defeating Hitler's army. Now the Allies had to march all the way to Berlin, the German capital.

In early June, Ike was delighted when General Marshall arranged for John Eisenhower to come to London for a two-week visit after his graduation from West Point. Ironically, John had graduated on June 6, D-Day.

When Ike heard the news of John's visit, he remarked, "How I look forward to seeing Johnny. It will be odd to see him as an officer of the Army! I'll burst with pride!"[1]

After John arrived in Europe, Ike took him everywhere he went, including the battlefront, and introduced him to Prime Minister Churchill.

Before returning home, John pleaded with his father to send him to France with one of the combat units. But Ike refused, knowing that if he did so, some officers would criticize him for interfering with army regulations.

After the invasion of the Normandy beaches, Prime Minister Churchill was gratified with the progress of the war and said that D-Day was "the most difficult and complicated operation that has ever taken place."[2]

Later, General Marshall arrived in England from Washington and, together with the Allied chiefs of staff, went to Normandy to inspect the progress of the invasion. All the officials were pleased that the Allies had ten divisions in France.

After D-Day, Ike faced some of his most nerve-wracking decisions, for he, along with other top officials, now had to coordinate the entire Allied invasion of Europe. They came up with the following plan: First, the Allies would capture the French coastal cities of Caen and Cherbourg. After these cities were conquered, they would march into Paris and seize the French capital from the Germans. Then they would cross the Rhine River and proceed on into the heart of Germany, thereby completely crushing the Nazis.

As Ike planned his military strategy, he analyzed the capabilities of the generals under his command. He knew that he could depend on the American generals, Omar Bradley and George Patton. Although he thought Patton was at times overzealous in attaining his objectives, Ike knew he could completely count on Bradley. He said of the general, "This officer is about the best-rounded, well-balanced senior officer that we have in the service. His judgments are always sound. . . . He is respected by British and Americans alike. . . . I feel that there is no position in the army that he could not fill with success."[3]

However, Ike was commander of the entire Allied forces, and he also had to work with the British and Free French generals.

Ike had mixed feelings about some of these other Allied army leaders. In fact, throughout the war, he often disagreed with the actions and policies of British General Montgomery and French General Charles de Gaulle. These men seemed to resent the fact that an American was the supreme commander. At the beginning of the war, they had been totally in charge of their nations' armed forces. Undoubtedly, they felt that General Eisenhower was a newcomer, because the Americans had entered the war long after the French and British.

Ike understood their resentment, but he also realized that he had been chosen as leader because of his tact and diplomacy. His good nature was at times pushed to its limit, when these free-spirited generals disagreed with him and wanted to go their own separate ways.

Soon after D-Day, Ike planned for General Montgomery and General Bradley to invade the cities of Caen and Cherbourg. Suddenly, events began to turn sour for the Allies. A hurricane developed that almost destroyed Omaha beach, making it impossible to supply the troops on shore for four days. In the storm, more than 300 Allied ships were sunk or grounded. After this delay, the Allies finally regrouped their forces and took the two French cities. But to accomplish this, they paid dearly in both men and supplies.

The next objective was to march to Paris. Everyone knew this would be an almost impossible task, because the enemy had strong defenses between the coast and the French capital. Indeed, it was extremely difficult, because en route the Allies fought one of the bloodiest battles of the war, the Battle of Falaise.

Ike said that this battle ". . . was unquestionably one of the great 'killing grounds' of any of the war areas. Roads, highways and fields were so choked with destroyed equipment and with dead men and animals that passage through the area was extremely difficult. . . ."[4]

After the grim Battle of Falaise, the American and British troops continued on their march toward Paris. On August 25, the Americans finally reached the outskirts of Paris. Ike said, ". . . after the capture of Paris, I notified General Charles de Gaulle that I hoped he, as the symbol of French resistance, would make an entrance before I had to go in. . . ."5

Eisenhower had somehow lost track of de Gaulle's whereabouts, because when his messenger tried to find General de Gaulle, he discovered that the general had arrived in Paris before the Americans.

The liberation of Paris turned out to be one of the most spectacular events of the war. The famous boulevard the Champs Élysées was lined with two million yelling, shouting Parisians, as General de Gaulle and his Free French troops marched by. Then the flame at the Tomb of the Unknown Soldier, built after the First World War, was relit. At one point on the parade route, General de Gaulle dramatically stopped the troops, and everyone sang the French national anthem, "La Marseillaise," as many Parisians wept with pride.

After the American troops arrived in Paris, Eisenhower met with General de Gaulle, who insisted that the Americans also march down the Champs Élysées. Ike's plan was for his troops to continue on with the war and go into battle that same day. But, because he knew it was important to the French and would also boost the soldiers' morale, Ike arranged for two of General Bradley's divisions to march through the streets of Paris. The Parisians greeted the Americans with as much enthusiasm as they had the Free French soldiers. The Yankees were their heroes too.

After Paris was taken from the Nazis, the whole world realized that the tide of the war had changed; the Allies were now winning. They had not only liberated Paris, but had also recaptured the port city of Marseilles in southern France.

At about this time, the Germans had another serious setback: the death of one of their ablest generals, Erwin Rommel. After supposedly being involved in a plot to murder Hitler, Rommel committed suicide. His death was a great loss to the Nazis' bid for power.

Ike was encouraged with the progress of the war, but he knew the Allies had a long fight ahead to reach Germany and the final defeat of the Nazis.

To strengthen the Allied position, Ike took personal command of the land battle and, at the same time, promoted General Bradley to command the 12th Army Group, making Bradley equal to General Montgomery, commander of the 21st Army Group. This action was later to cause a conflict between these two generals.

One of Ike's major problems at this time was that he and General Montgomery had very different ideas about how to go about invading Germany. Ike intended to enter Germany on a "broad-front advance"; in other words, all the Allied troops marching into Germany together. Monty, on the other hand, favored a "single thrust" plan, or a quick drive by his troops, first to the Ruhr industrial area, and then to Berlin. Because of this disagreement, Ike sometimes felt that Monty delayed in following his orders.

After taking Paris on August 25, the Allies were gaining ground until December 1944, when the Nazis tried to make their last desperate comeback in a breakthrough in the Allied lines in the Ardennes forest in Belgium. Hitler had planned this attack for many months and had caught the Allies completely off guard. This assault was later named the Battle of the Bulge, because when the Germans attacked the Allied line, a fifty-mile bulge formed in their line of defense. The Germans' aim at this time was to push the Allies back to the English Channel. Being very low on fuel for their tanks and planes, the Nazis intended first to capture the American gasoline and other supplies, and then to push on and capture the city of Antwerp, a major Allied port.

The Battle of the Bulge began on December 16, and Ike received the news that he had been promoted to five-star general, or general of the army, on December 15. Although pleased to receive this great honor, he was too involved in the war to worry about a fifth star on his uniform.

In the Battle of the Bulge, after the first German attack, the Allied troops were forced to retreat. The Nazis were able to capture two Allied regiments of 7,000 men.

The situation looked extremely serious on December 19, when Ike met with Air Marshal Tedder and Generals Bradley, Patton, and Devers at Verdun. At this meeting, Ike said, "The present situation is to be regarded as one of opportunity for us and not a disaster. There will be only cheerful faces at this conference table."[6] Optimistic by nature, Eisenhower inspired others to be hopeful.

Even though he tried to be confident about the situation, Ike was extremely worried. He issued one of his few "Orders of the Day," which stated, ". . . Let everyone hold before him a single thought—to destroy the enemy on the ground, in the air, everywhere—destroy him! United in this determination and with unshakable faith in the cause for which we fight, we will, with God's help, go forward to our greatest victory."[7]

But the Allied position worsened when Bastogne, a city in Belgium held by the Americans, was completely surrounded by the Nazis. Ike knew that if the Americans did not hold Bastogne, the Germans would be able to march to Antwerp.

Determined to stop the Nazis, Ike gave standing orders, "Hold Bastogne!" In spite of this, the German troops got closer and closer and soon demanded that the Americans surrender this key city. Fortunately, General Anthony McAuliffe and his 101st Airborne Division saved the day. When the Germans contacted McAuliffe to surrender, he simply said, "Nuts."[8]

The Germans didn't know what he meant, until a translator told them it could be translated as, "Go to hell!"

After McAuliffe's troops arrived, the Americans were able to stop the Germans at Bastogne.

During this last-ditch try to defeat the Allies, the Nazis used every trick they knew. Indeed, they even circulated rumors that someone planned to kill Generals Eisenhower, Bradley, and Montgomery. In fact, once Ike had a very close call. He had intended to board a train to Brussels on December 26 to meet General Montgomery. He missed the train and caught one the following day. The train he had planned to take was bombed.

A little later, because of death threats, Ike was forced to stay in his quarters for several days. Finally, tiring of his confinement, he shouted, "Hell's fire, I'm going out for a walk. If anyone wants to shoot me, he can go right ahead. . . ."[9]

Another way the Nazis tried to deceive the Allies was to have English-speaking Germans dressed in American and British uniforms infiltrate behind the Allied lines and give the troops false information. When the Allies discovered these treacherous tactics, they tightened security, adding additional checkpoints everywhere. At these stations the guards asked the soldiers questions about their hometowns and who won the World Series, testing them to see if they were really Americans. The guards also spoke to the soldiers in American slang to see if they understood. Everyone was questioned; even General Bradley was stopped at one checkpoint.

The Battle of the Bulge continued on through December, and Ike spent a bleak Christmas. He wrote Mamie, ending by saying, "Well, Sweet, I do hope you and John have a nice Christmas. For me there will be none—but that's part of this dirty business. But next year we'll be together if God is good to us. Loads of love."[10]

After Christmas in 1944, the Allies intended to make a counterattack on the Germans. Ike planned for General Patton's forces to attack from the south and General Montgomery's forces from the north. But, unfortunately, on December 30, Monty was not ready.

Ike and Monty had agreed to attack on January 1, 1945, but on December 30, Monty's chief of staff came to Ike at SHAEF headquarters saying that Monty would not attack until January 3. Ike felt that Monty was purposely delaying and disobeying his orders. He thought that Montgomery wanted sole command of the whole operation.

Ike could hardly control his temper when he met with Monty's chief of staff. He was so furious that while he was talking to Monty's aide, he tore his handkerchief into bits under his desk.

Finally, Ike drafted a letter to Monty, demanding that he live up to his promises, or Ike would ask Prime Minister Churchill to relieve him of command. Monty's aide begged Ike not to send the letter and promised to talk to the general. Ike agreed not to send it. Later, he received a letter from Monty stating, "You can rely on me and all under my command to go all out one hundred percent to implement your plan."[11]

After this delay, the Allied counterattack began on January 2, with Patton's and Montgomery's soldiers ruthlessly pounding the Nazi troops. During early January, the fighting continued unabated until the tide of the battle turned, and the Allies overpowered the Nazi army. On January 13, the Germans finally called for a general retreat.

The Battle of the Bulge proved to be one of the bloodiest battles of the war in Europe. When it finally ended, the Nazis had lost 100,000 troops and the Allies 81,000; the majority of these were Americans. Fortunately for the Allies, this battle marked the beginning of the end of Nazi control of Europe.

After this devastating battle, Eisenhower's only thought was to move rapidly into Germany and conquer Hitler and the Nazis forever.

CHAPTER NINE

"The Mission of This Allied Force Was Fulfilled"

After the Battle of the Bulge, Ike felt that it was time for the Americans and British to coordinate their strategy with the Soviet Union. Ever since the Battle of Stalingrad in 1942, the Soviets had been winning battles against the Nazis on the eastern front. In January, Ike sent Air Marshal Arthur Tedder to Moscow to discuss war plans with the Soviets, as all three Allies prepared to enter Germany.

Now Ike's first priority was to march to the heart of Germany. In order to do this, the Americans and British had to first cross the Rhine River. On March 7, General Bradley's troops crossed the bridge over the Rhine at Remagen. Bradley phoned Ike while Ike hosted a dinner for the division commanders of the American airborne forces.

Ike later said, "That was one of my happy moments of the war. This was completely unforeseen. We were across the Rhine, on a permanent bridge; the traditional defensive barrier to the heart of Germany was pierced." [1]

After crossing the Rhine, the Allies marched toward the heart of Germany through the industrial area of the Ruhr valley. During this march, Ike's troops uncovered some unexpected evidence of Nazi cruelty. First, General

Patton's troops found Nazi treasure hidden in a deep salt mine—hundreds of valuable paintings and other art objects, and an estimated 250 million dollars' worth of gold bars. These had been stolen by the Nazis in the countries they conquered.

The same day that Ike visited the salt mines, he and his troops marched into a concentration camp near the town of Gotha. Ike had received many reports of the horror of the camps where the Nazis had put to death millions of Jews and other prisoners, but he had never seen one. After visiting the camp, he remarked, ". . . I never felt able to describe my emotional reactions when I first came face-to-face with indisputable evidence of Nazi brutality. . . . I have never at any other time experienced an equal sense of shock. . . ."[2]

Ike visited the entire camp, because he felt it his duty to see it firsthand. Then he could report back to the United States the true horror of these places, in case the American people thought that the stories of the Nazi brutality were exaggerated. He wrote, "I felt that the evidence should be immediately placed before the American and British publics in a fashion that would leave no room for cynical doubt."[3]

After touring the concentration camp, Eisenhower sent messages to Washington and London urging the governments to send newspaper correspondents and government officials to Germany to cover the story.

Later, after visiting another such camp, Ike said, "I want every American unit not actually in the front line to see this place. We are told that the American soldier does not know what he is fighting for. Now, at least, he will know what he is fighting against."[4]

After seeing these shocking places, Ike knew that he had to lead the Allies on to victory to rid the world of the Nazis' evil power.

Generals Eisenhower, Bradley, and others—including many American soldiers—visited the site of the Nazi concentration camp at Gotha, Germany.

After the Allies crossed the Rhine, Ike faced his biggest headache of the entire war—which of the Allied troops should capture Berlin. The Americans, the British, and the Soviets all hoped to arrive there first. Although each country wanted the privilege of seizing the German capital, each wished to pursue a different goal after the war was over. The United States wanted a secure Europe built around a new non-Nazi Germany. Thus, President Roosevelt wished to continue the alliance with Britain and the Soviet Union. On the other hand, British Prime Minister Churchill felt that after Hitler was defeated, there would be no reason for the Americans and British to cooperate with the Soviets.

In spite of the Allies' differences, it had already been agreed upon at the Yalta Conference, when Roosevelt, Churchill, and Soviet head of state Joseph Stalin met in February 1945, that no matter which country entered Berlin first, the Allies would divide the city into three sectors: one for each of the Allies—the United States, Great Britain, and the Soviet Union. Later, France was added to the group, and Berlin was divided into four sectors.

Some officials believed that the country that had contributed most to winning the war should have the privilege of taking the capital. The Soviets argued that they had the most casualties, 20 million people. They had also defeated the German army in the eastern section. The British contended that they fought alone against Hitler in 1940 and 1941, and the Americans claimed that they had contributed the most military supplies.

Eisenhower worried for weeks over this problem. He knew it was up to him to make the momentous decision of which nation should seize Berlin. He realized that he could not please everyone, and it was his duty to take into consideration what would be best for all sides.

Complicating matters further, Ike's generals could not agree on a solution. General Patton wanted Ike to hold

Montgomery's forces on the Rhine, and let his troops (Patton's) reach Berlin first. Monty, on the other hand, wanted Patton stopped and Patton's supplies sent to him; then he would make a dash to Berlin.

Ike was trying to solve this dilemma, when a fierce rivalry developed between General Bradley and General Montgomery. When Bradley got word that Monty might once again be in charge of all the Allied ground forces, he complained to Ike, saying, "You must know after what has happened I cannot serve under Montgomery. If he is to be put in command of all ground forces, you must send me home, for if Montgomery goes in over me, I will have lost the confidence of my command."

Ike said, ". . . I thought you were the one person I could count on for doing anything I asked you to."

Bradley replied, "You can, Ike. I've enjoyed every bit of my service with you. But this is one thing I cannot take."[5]

Finally, Ike decided to let Bradley keep his own command.

Ike spent many wakeful nights over all of these problems. Then after weeks of deliberation, he finally decided that the Soviets should capture Berlin. His decision was based on two main factors. First, the Soviets were actually closer to the capital. Their armies were thirty-five miles from Berlin, while the Allied troops were fifty miles away. Second, General Bradley told Eisenhower that he estimated that in order to take Berlin, there would be 100,000 American casualties. This was probably the main reason Ike decided to let the Soviets go in first. Unless it was absolutely necessary, he couldn't bear to think of losing thousands of American lives at the very end of the war. His decision would shape history for years to come.

After the Allies crossed the Rhine, and the Soviet army was descending from the east, Berlin was surrounded on all sides. Then the Nazi army began to disintegrate.

Thousands of German soldiers streamed back from the Russian front and began giving themselves up to the Americans and British. The Nazis felt that they would receive better treatment from the Western Allies, because early in the war the Nazis had marched through Russia massacring millions of people. By April the Americans and British had captured more than a million prisoners.

While the end of the war was approaching in Europe, an important event occurred in the United States. On April 12, 1945, President Roosevelt died. Ike heard the news in the middle of the night, while he was staying at Patton's headquarters. The three generals—Eisenhower, Bradley, and Patton—got up, and in their bathrobes, discussed until morning what this event would mean. How would the new president, Harry Truman, handle the remainder of the war?

The end of the war came rapidly. After the Soviet army surrounded and entered Berlin, the city was in flames, with thousands of people fleeing in desperation. Hitler, the once mighty führer, was a completely disheartened man. In his luxurious bunker in Berlin, his new wife, Eva Braun, took poison, then Hitler shot himself. But before he committed suicide, Hitler encouraged other leaders to follow his example and take their own lives. Hitler said, "The German people have not shown themselves worthy of the führer, and he can only die. The future belongs to the strong—to the East."[6]

After Hitler's suicide on April 30, what remained of the German government fell into the hands of Admiral Karl Doenitz. Finally, Berlin surrendered to the Soviet Union on May 2, 1945.

On May 4, Ike issued the following statement to the Allies, ". . . On land, sea, and air the Germans are thoroughly whipped. Their only recourse is to surrender."[7]

At the last moment, German General Himmler made every effort to surrender to the Western Allies, because he knew his troops would receive better treatment from them than from the Soviets. Himmler pleaded to both Eisenhower and Prime Minister Churchill to be allowed to give up to the British and Americans. In fact, just before the surrender, Churchill called Ike eight times one night trying to solve the problem. Finally, exasperated, Ike told Churchill, with regard to the Germans giving up to the west, "You wrap it up in diplomatic language and tell him [Himmler] to go to hell."[8]

But later, Nazi General Jodl still stalled for time. Finally, on May 7, Ike told his assistant, General Walter Bedell Smith, "You tell them [the Germans] that 48 hours from midnight tonight, I will close my lines on the Western front so no more Germans can get through."[9]

Thus on May 7, the Germans surrendered at Reims. Ike was still so furious because of all the stalling for time, that he refused to go to the surrender ceremony. He sent General Smith to represent him.

Although Ike was not at the ceremony, he was nearby in his office. And after General Smith told him that the surrender papers had been signed, he went in and confronted General Jodl.

Eisenhower later said, "I asked him through the interpreter if he thoroughly understood all provisions of the document he had signed."[10]

Jodl replied, "Ja."

Ike continued, "You will, officially and personally, be held responsible if the terms of this surrender are violated, including its provisions for German commanders to appear in Berlin at the moment set by the Russian High Command to accomplish formal surrender to that government. That is all."[11]

After the surrender, Ike said that his greatest moment was on May 7, 1945, when he dispatched the following message to his British and American superiors in Washington and London: "The mission of this Allied force was fulfilled."[12]

At the very end, Ike phoned General Bradley at the front and said, "Make sure that all firing stops at midnight of the eighth."[13]

Finally the war in Europe was over.

★ ★ ★ ★ ★

After the surrender, Ike issued a solemn Victory Order of the Day, which called for no celebrations. It read, "The route you have traveled through hundreds of miles is marked by the graves of former comrades. Each of the fallen died as a member of the team to which you belong, bound together by a common love of liberty and a refusal to submit to enslavement. . . . Every man, every woman of every nation here represented has served according to his or her ability, and the efforts of each have contributed to the outcome. This we shall remember—and in doing so we shall be revering each honored grave, and be sending comfort to the loved ones of comrades who could not live to see this day."[14]

At the end, Ike refused to let the American troops celebrate, although people in many cities in Europe and America hailed VE day (Victory in Europe) with shouting, drinking, and parties. Eisenhower merely thanked God that the war in Europe was finally over. He prayed that the world would never again know such evil forces as Hitler and the Nazi regime.

After the German surrender, Ike was surprised to receive a cordial letter from General Montgomery, with whom he had disagreed so much during the war. It read in part, "Dear Ike . . . I suppose we shall soon begin to run our own affairs . . . what a privilege and an honor it has been to serve under you. I owe much to your wise guidance and kindly forbearance. . . . I do not suppose I am an easy subordinate; I like to go my own way. . . . But you have kept me on the rails in difficult and stormy times, and have taught me much. . . . Your very devoted friend, Monty."[15]

A month after the Nazis surrendered, Ike returned to London, where he received a hero's welcome. Before he went back to the United States, he gave a speech at London Guildhall on June 12, in which he said, ". . . No man alone could have brought about this result. Had I possessed the military skill of a Marlborough, the wisdom of Solomon, the understanding of Lincoln, I still would have been helpless without the loyalty, vision, and generosity of thousands upon thousands of British and Americans. . . . My most cherished hope is that . . . neither my country nor yours need ever again summon its sons and daughters from their peaceful pursuits to face the tragedies of battle. . . ."[16]

Eisenhower had won his crusade in Europe, but at a great price. After seeing firsthand the death, destruction, and grief of war, he truly believed that war was hell on earth. His hatred for the Nazis had forced him to put a supreme effort into winning the war. At the beginning, it looked as if the Nazis would rule the world. But the Allies had pulled together and won. Eisenhower would never get over the bitter taste of war and vowed he must do everything in his power to ensure world peace for future generations.

CHAPTER TEN

Ike Promised to "Think the Matter Over"

In June 1945, Ike received a hero's welcome in both Europe and the United States. He had concentrated so hard on fighting the war that he was completely oblivious to his own popularity. Indeed, Ike wanted to give others credit. In a speech in London he said, "Humility must always be the portion of any man who receives acclaim earned in the blood of his followers and the sacrifices of his friends."[1]

When he arrived in London, he rode in an open carriage through the streets, as spectators greeted him with tremendous enthusiasm. Then he went to Paris and again experienced an overwhelming welcome.

When Ike arrived in Washington, he greeted Mamie affectionately. He was delighted to see her after such a long separation.

Later in New York City, Ike's car drove down Broadway in a ticker-tape parade, as thousands of people lined the sidewalks shouting and yelling. From there, he proceeded to West Point, then to Kansas City, Missouri, and finally to his hometown, Abilene. By now, Ike was so well known by the American people that he seemed like an old friend who had gone off to war and suddenly returned a hero.

*In Kansas City, Missouri, in June 1945,
General Eisenhower received a hero's welcome and
a ticker-tape parade planned in his honor.*

Although World War II ended in Europe in May 1945, it raged on in the Pacific. Since he was still on active duty, Eisenhower had to return to Europe. Although no longer supreme allied commander, he was still commander of all American troops in Europe. He also became military governor of Germany.

After Ike returned to Germany, Premier Joseph Stalin invited him to visit the Soviet Union. At that time Stalin wanted a friendly relationship with the United States, since after the war, the United States and the Soviet Union had emerged as the two major world powers.

On this trip Ike was accompanied by his son, John, and General Lucius Clay. In Moscow, Marshal Gregory Zhukov, a Soviet official with whom Ike had recently worked in Berlin on the Allied Control Council, met Eisenhower and his group. Ike and Zhukov had become good friends in Berlin, and both men sincerely wanted to promote world peace.

Later in Moscow, General Ike met Premier Stalin and visited many historical sites. On Ike's last night in the Soviet Union, American Ambassador Averell Harriman gave a large banquet for Eisenhower and some of the Soviet officials. Just as everyone sat down for dinner, Ambassador Harriman received a message and excused himself. Before he left, he asked Ike to entertain the gathering until he returned. Ike and other Americans present gave toast after toast, and then one speech after another. Ike hoped that the ambassador would return before all the guests left.

When Mr. Harriman returned to the table, he announced that the Japanese had surrendered to the Allies and the war was over in the Pacific. Ike was overjoyed. It was also announced that just before the surrender, the Americans had dropped atomic bombs on Hiroshima and Nagasaki. Although Ike had always been opposed to atomic warfare, he was now thankful that all fighting had ceased throughout the world.

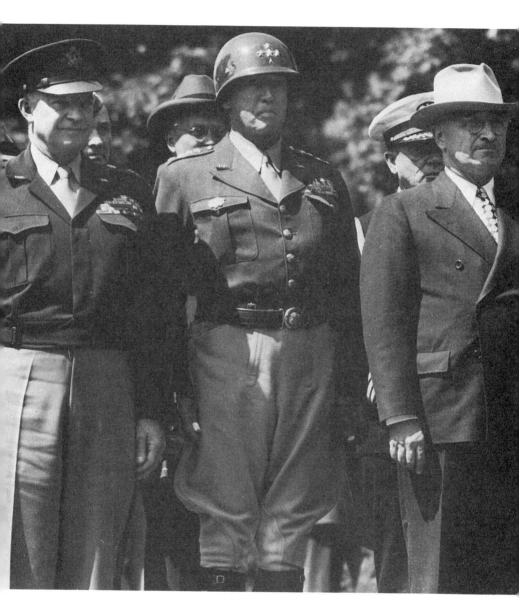

*Eisenhower, Patton, and Truman
watched the flag-raising ceremony
in Berlin on July 28, 1945.*

Later that year, Ike was recalled to the states, where-upon President Truman appointed him army chief of staff. Ike felt that the job as chief of staff was anti-climactic after his years in Europe. His major problem was the huge task of disbanding the army after the war. Later, he had to deal with the overwhelming dilemma of unifying the armed services into one huge department. In 1946, an act of Congress ordered that the army, navy, and air force become the Department of Defense.

Shortly after the war, several important events occurred in Ike's personal life. He and Mamie were both delighted when their son, John, married Barbara Jean Thompson, the daughter of a colonel.

That same year, Ike was saddened to hear of the death of his old friend General George Patton, who was killed in a jeep accident in Germany shortly after the war. The two men had been friends for over twenty years.

One day in his Washington office, while Ike was army chief of staff, he received a visit from Thomas Watson, an acquaintance who was a trustee of Columbia University and president of IBM. At this meeting, Mr. Watson asked Ike if he would possibly consider becoming president of Columbia.

During the discussion, Eisenhower told Watson that he thought of himself as a soldier rather than a scholar. Ike said that maybe Mr. Watson had him confused with his brother Milton, who was president of Kansas State College.

Mr. Watson replied, "We already have enough scholars . . . what we need is a leader of the university."[2]

After talking it over with Mamie and giving the proposal serious consideration, Ike decided that he would accept the offer to become president of Columbia University. In 1948, he turned the position of army chief of staff over to his old friend General Omar Bradley, and suddenly became a civilian.

During his final leave before he retired as chief of staff, Ike wrote a book about his war experiences, *Crusade In Europe.* It was published in 1948 and soon became a best seller. The book was later translated into a number of foreign languages.

During the war, Ike had not been able to save much money, because of the demands of his army career. But now after the success of his book and the income it earned, Ike and Mamie were able to purchase a farm in Gettysburg, Pennsylvania.

All her married life, Mamie had complained that she had never had a home of her own. Now her dream for their own home was beginning to come true. The farm they bought needed almost every type of repair. The farmhouse had to be rebuilt from the ground up, and the farm itself needed replanting and cultivating. In spite of this, Ike and Mamie felt fortunate that they could build a home of their own.

Ike's whole family attended his installation as president of Columbia University. At the reception, his brother Edgar remarked, "Father would have liked this, Ike, even better than seeing you a general."[3] Ike remembered his parent's strong opposition to his army career.

At Columbia, Ike and Mamie lived in a mansion in Morningside Heights reserved for the president of the university. Since the huge house lacked a homey atmosphere, for a cozy retreat, Mamie made a penthouse out of a room that housed a water tank. From this rooftop room, Ike and Mamie could relax in the evening and view the lights of the city. Ike even had time to take up painting as a hobby, and he sometimes used Mamie as a model. After working hard on his first portrait of her, he looked at the painting and remarked that it was "weird and wonderful to behold, and we all laughed heartily."[4]

Ike and Mamie were enjoying their life at Columbia when an important event occurred in their lives—the birth

*Eisenhower temporarily retired from
military life and became president of
Columbia University in New York City in 1948.*

of their first grandchild. Dwight David Eisenhower II was born at West Point, where his father, John, and mother, Barbara, lived.

Although Ike enjoyed his years at Columbia, he sometimes had difficulty carrying out his duties at the university because he was often called to Washington by government officials seeking his opinion on numerous military problems.

Often frustrated by trying to satisfy government officials as well as his colleagues at Columbia, Ike was open to a change in his career. Then one day while he was still president of Columbia, Ike had an unusual call. He and Mamie were traveling by train to Heidelberg College in Ohio on university business. During a stop in a small town, a railway employee gave Ike a message that President Truman wished to speak to him on the telephone.

When Ike placed the call at the next train station, Mr. Truman told him that the North Atlantic Treaty Organization had met and wanted him to become the commander of NATO. Mr. Truman said to Ike that he really wanted him to accept this appointment.

In 1948, NATO had been established by a group of twelve Western European nations, the United States, and Canada. These countries felt that the Soviet Union's expansion in Eastern Europe was becoming a serious threat to their safety.

At first, Ike was reluctant to take the job with NATO, because he knew that Mamie was enjoying their life at Columbia. Then Ike thought of his continuing desire to do everything in his power to ensure peace in Europe. He felt that the job with NATO might be a means to this end. He told President Truman that he would gladly take the position, if the president thought he would be the best man for the job.

Later that year, with President Truman's encouragement, Ike resigned his position at Columbia University, and he and Mamie prepared to leave for Europe. Shortly after he decided to take the job at NATO, Ike told a friend, "I'm a soldier and this is a call to duty. . . . My objective will not be to prepare for war, but to make sure there won't be any."5 With bitter memories of the devastation after World War II, Ike wanted to do his best to promote peace.

In France, Ike and Mamie moved into a lovely chateau near the town of Versailles, outside of Paris. During his years as commander of NATO, Ike enjoyed touring many of the European cities he had seen during the war. He was pleased to note that they were all being rebuilt. In some of the cities Ike visited, he was still hailed as a war hero.

During the time he was commander of NATO, Eisenhower's biggest problem was getting the member countries to admit West Germany into the organization. It was not admitted into the organization until 1955, after Ike was no longer commander.

While Ike was in Europe, he received thousands of letters from people in the United States urging him to return home and run for president. That year songwriter Irving Berlin wrote a song titled, "I Like Ike," for the Broadway play, *Call Me Madam*. Before long, everyone began humming this tune.

Republican Senator Henry Cabot Lodge visited Eisenhower in Paris and begged him to become a candidate in the 1952 presidential election. At this meeting, Ike asked Senator Lodge why he wasn't running for president himself.

The senator replied, "Because I cannot be elected. . . . You are the only one who can be elected by the Republicans to the Presidency. You must permit the use of your name in the upcoming primaries."6

Finally at the end of the conversation, Ike promised to think the matter over.

Jacqueline Cochran, a well-known writer and aviator, also visited Ike in Paris. She brought with her a movie of a rally that had been held in Madison Square Garden to draft Ike for president. Fifteen thousand people attended. When Ike saw the film, he said, "It was a moving experience to witness . . . such a huge crowd—to realize that everyone present was enthusiastically supporting me for the highest office of the land."[7] He was truly astonished by his own popularity.

In March 1952, New Hampshire held the first primary election for president. Senator Robert Taft of Ohio was the Republican nominee, and Eisenhower's name was not even on the ballot. Some people did not even know whether Ike was a Republican or a Democrat. However, before the election, two old friends of Ike's, General Lucius Clay and Senator Lodge, told the voters that Ike was indeed a Republican, because he had voted for that party since 1948 when he left the army. In that primary, Ike received a majority of Republican votes. Later, in the Minnesota primary, Ike's name was not on the ballot either, but he again won the election by receiving a majority of write-in votes.

Indeed, the American people were actually begging Ike to run for president. Although reluctant to do so, Ike finally decided that if so many people had confidence in him, he must become a candidate.

Ike said, "I was, of course, a political novice. But because of special experiences in my past life, I was probably more acutely aware than the average citizen of the complexities, anxieties and burdens of the life led by a head of government. . . ."[8]

Suddenly Ike's attitude changed. He knew it was time to return home and become a full-fledged candidate. So in June, he resigned his position at NATO and flew home. After arriving in the United States from Paris, Ike first flew to Abilene to lay the cornerstone of the Eisenhower Foundation, honoring the fighting men in World War II. While there, he gave his first speech of the 1952 presidential campaign. With Mamie's encouragement, Ike became enthusiastic about the possibility of being president. Now he was eager to get in there and fight to win the election.

CHAPTER ELEVEN

"Ike and Mamie — the People's Future Is with You in '52"

At the Republican convention of 1952, held in Chicago, Eisenhower and Senator Taft were the two Republican hopefuls for president in the November election. By now, Ike, encouraged by many devoted supporters, was a willing candidate and had many delegates working on his behalf. Senator Taft had always been the favorite candidate of the leaders of the Republican party.

The opening speaker at the convention happened to be Ike's former commanding officer, General Douglas MacArthur. For many years, Ike's relationship with his old commander had not been cordial. In the past, the two generals had exchanged backhanded compliments. MacArthur reportedly said that Ike was "the best clerk who ever served under me."[1] And Ike remarked that he had enjoyed "studying dramatics" under MacArthur.[2]

General MacArthur had been in the headlines in 1951, when President Truman relieved him of command in Korea because MacArthur advocated expanding the Korean War into Red China, an idea that the president vigorously opposed.

When Ike learned that MacArthur had been relieved of command, he remarked, "When you put on a uniform there are certain inhibitions you accept."[3] In other words, a general, while in the service, cannot openly disagree with the president of the United States.

When it came time to vote on the first ballot, Eisenhower received 595 votes, 9 votes short of winning, and Taft received 500. Then the Minnesota delegation changed its nineteen votes from its favorite-son candidate, Harold Stassen, to Ike, and he won easily on the first ballot. Eisenhower picked as his running mate thirty-nine-year-old Senator Richard Nixon of California.

In his acceptance speech at the convention, Ike said, ". . . I accept their [Republicans] summons to lead a crusade, a crusade for freedom in America and freedom in the world. . . ."[4] Ike liked to think in terms of a crusade, almost a holy war. During World War II, he had led a crusade against the Nazis. Now he intended to lead a crusade for world peace.

After he won the primary, Ike was anxious to get on with the campaign and the November election. Everywhere Ike campaigned, huge crowds of supporters turned out to hear him. Many people carried signs reading, "We like Ike," "Vote Right for Ike," and "Ike and Mamie—the People's Future Is with You in '52."

Eisenhower ran against the Democratic governor from Illinois, Adlai Stevenson. The campaign was unusual for two reasons. It was the first presidential campaign to be televised, and the last where candidates made "whistle-stops," short visits to small towns by railroad, making speeches from a platform at the back of the train.

At times Ike became worn out from the vigorous campaign his advisors planned for him. Ike and Mamie spent election night at the Commodore Hotel in New York City. Ike's brothers Arthur, Earl, and Milton were with them as they watched the election returns on television in the hotel room. Toward midnight the returns came in favoring Ike. Ike was relieved that the election was over.

At this time, the United States was fighting in the Korean War. The war had begun in 1950, when the Communist North Koreans invaded South Korea. In 1951, United Nations forces, including United States troops, were sent to Korea to settle the dispute. Ike felt that the war had dragged on too long, and during his presidential campaign in a speech in Detroit, he said ". . . I announced my intention . . . to go to Korea before the following January to determine for myself what the conditions were in that unhappy country."5

By election time in 1952, this war had escalated, with American casualties reaching 21,000 killed and 91,000 wounded.

Ike kept his promise, and between his nomination and his inauguration, he flew to Korea to evaluate the war situation. Upon arriving there, he met his son, John, who was an army major serving at the front. Then Ike traveled around Korea to observe the progress of the war. When he returned home, Ike promised that after he became president he would make every effort to end the war.

On Inauguration Day in 1953, President Truman and President-elect Eisenhower rode together to the Capitol in a limousine. Ike's relationship with President Truman had become strained at times, because of Ike's criticism of the Korean War. However, on this day, they seemed on friendly terms.

Ike enjoyed the five-hour-long parade before the inauguration, which included West Point cadets, hundreds of marching bands, and even a parade of cowboys, reminiscent of Ike's early days in Abilene at the turn of the century.

After the swearing-in ceremony at the Capitol, Ike offered a prayer he had composed himself, which read in

After winning the election in 1952,
President-elect Eisenhower visited Korea
to evaluate the situation there firsthand.
Always a soldier, Eisenhower ate with
members of the U.S. Infantry Division.

part, "Give us, we pray, the power to discern clearly right from wrong, and allow all our words and actions to be governed thereby, and by the laws of this land. . . ."[6]

A few days after Eisenhower became president, he realized that from now on even his best friends would treat him almost like a stranger. He said, "I've just learned a lesson from Omar Bradley. He addressed me over the phone as 'Mr. President' . . . a man who for forty years had called me 'Ike,' as I had called him 'Brad.' His salutation put me on notice. . . . I would . . . to a very definite degree be separated from all others, including my oldest friends. . . ."[7] Ike suddenly realized that being president of the United States could be a lonely job.

Eisenhower's background had been good preparation for his presidential years. By now he was confident that he could lead diverse groups of men under difficult circumstances. As supreme commander in Europe, he had been able to get the Allies to form a team and work together to win the war. He knew how difficult it had been to persuade such forceful personalities as Generals Montgomery, Patton, and De Gaulle to pull together to defeat the Nazis. He realized that now these skills would be put to the ultimate test. His first job was to choose a cabinet to help him execute his duties, and he also had to maintain good relations with Congress, the Supreme Court, and the governments of many foreign nations. Ike realized that the job ahead of him was even tougher than that of being supreme allied commander.

Eisenhower's first priority as president was to keep his promise and end the Korean War. To put an end to the war, Eisenhower and Secretary of State John Foster Dulles conducted many negotiations with South Korean President Syngman Rhee. Finally, a truce was signed on July 27, 1953, at Panmunjom, South Korea.

After the armistice, Ike felt satisfied that he had reached his first goal as president: to bring a peaceful

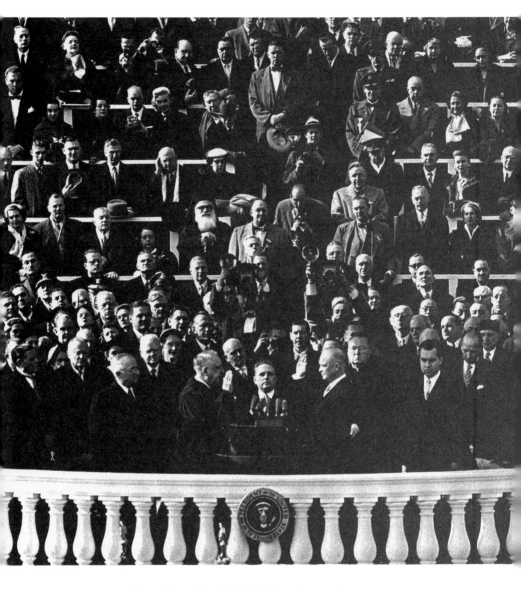

President Dwight D. Eisenhower is sworn in.
He soon realized even his
personal life would never be the same.

settlement of the Korean War. He also urged Congress to spend $200,000,000 to help rebuild Korea. Later, at the end of his term of office, Ike looked back on the Korean peace agreement as one of his greatest achievements as president.

With the horror of World War II still burning in his memory, Ike was ready to move ahead with his crusade for world peace. He wanted to reverse the bitter feelings some nations had toward the United States because of its use of the atomic bomb in Japan at the end of the war. With no major wars in progress, Ike hoped that the world could make constructive use of atomic power. For these reasons, in December 1953, he went to the United Nations with his "Atoms for Peace" proposal, saying that the United States' stockpile of atomic weapons was larger than the total explosive power of all the bombs used in World War II.

Ike hoped to eliminate the fear of atomic warfare throughout the world. He proposed that the Americans, Soviets, and British contribute from their nuclear stockpiles to a United Nations agency for peaceful uses of atomic energy.

In his speech before the United Nations, Eisenhower said, "The United States pledges before you—and therefore before the world—its determination to help solve the fearful atomic dilemma—to devote its entire heart and mind to find the way which the miraculous inventiveness of man shall not be dedicated to his death, but consecrated to his life."[8]

While Ike was working hard to promote world peace, other events were happening at home. In the United States Congress, Republican Senator Joseph McCarthy of Wisconsin was causing great dissension by claiming that there were hundreds of card-carrying Communists working in government jobs and in other areas, especially in the film industry. McCarthy, with the support of other senators, held hearings to try to oust these presumed Communist sympathizers. As McCarthy's power grew, many people in and out of government felt that he was conducting a "witch hunt." In other words, he was trying to convict people of being Communists on very slight evidence.

Ike felt that McCarthy's actions should be settled in Congress and that it was not his problem. After several years, McCarthy's investigations went too far when he began questioning army officers. Finally in 1954, he was censured by the United States Senate for conduct "contrary to Senatorial traditions."9

Ike was undoubtedly relieved when the McCarthy hearings ended. Some Americans criticized him for his hands-off attitude about McCarthy.

In the summer of 1955, Eisenhower was invited to participate in the first post-World War II summit meeting in Geneva, Switzerland. As he flew to Geneva for the conference, Eisenhower continued thinking of how he could encourage world peace.

When he arrived at the airport in Geneva, Ike told the press, "Eleven years ago, I came to Europe with an army, a navy and an air force. This time, I come with something more powerful . . . the aspirations of Americans for peace."10

In Geneva, Eisenhower met with Nikolai Bulganin and Nikita Khrushchev representing the Soviet Union, Anthony Eden of Great Britain, and Edgar Fauré of France. Ike described his Russian counterpart, Chairman Khrushchev, as "rotund and amiable, but with a will of iron only slightly concealed."11 Ike knew he had to be diplomatic with Khrushchev, but he was determined not to let the Soviet official get the upper hand.

The first evening, during dinner, Eisenhower told Khrushchev that it was "essential [to] find some way of controlling the threat of the thermonuclear bomb. You know, we both have enough weapons to wipe out the entire northern hemisphere from fallout alone."

Khrushchev replied, "We get your dust, you get our dust, the winds blow and nobody's safe."[12]

Ike agreed.

The next day in a speech at the conference, Eisenhower initiated his policy of "Open Skies." He said, "I have been searching my heart and mind for something that I could say here that could convince everyone of the great sincerity of the United States . . ."[13] As if predicting an evil omen, a roar of thunder and a flash of lightning extinguished all the lights and the sound system in the room.

After the lights came back on, Eisenhower continued, saying that the Open Skies policy called on the United States and the Soviet Union to grant each other permission to fly over and photograph each other's military sites. Ike felt that in this way both countries would better understand the other's military situation, and there would be no reason for espionage.

Chairman Khrushchev strongly disagreed with Ike over the Open Skies policy. He told Eisenhower that these flights were the same as spying, and that they would give the United States an advantage over the Soviet Union, because the United States would learn too much about that country's military bases.

Ike again urged Khrushchev to at least give the Open Skies policy a try. Sadly, however, he realized that Khrushchev would never agree.

At that time, Ike feared that the Soviets had many spies in the United States, and that our government knew little about the Soviet defense system because of the tight security around their military installations.

At the end of the conference, Ike realized that little had been accomplished, but he hoped it was the beginning of a better understanding between the Americans and the Soviets. At least a bit of warmth developed between the two countries—Khrushchev and Bulganin asked Eisenhower to invite them to visit the United States.

Back in Washington, during a discussion of the Open Skies policy with some of his colleagues, Ike said, "I'll give it one shot. Then if they don't accept it, we'll fly the U-2."[14] A very light plane that could be flown high over land for the purpose of aerial photography, the U-2 had been secretly built, at the government's request, at Lockheed Aircraft Corporation.

At the end of his first term as president, Ike felt that his crusade for peace was beginning to work, and he wanted more time to promote his plans. So in spite of a recent heart attack, he decided to run for a second term.

At the Republican convention in San Francisco in the summer of 1956, Ike was unanimously elected on the first ballot, again choosing Richard Nixon as his running mate, although some people advised him to dump Nixon.

As if to test Ike's peacemaking ability, events happened between the convention and the election in November that severely shocked the world. The first confrontation occurred when both Poland and Hungary rebelled against the Soviet Union. Because Chairman Khrushchev had denounced the criminal behavior of his predecessor, Joseph Stalin, in a private speech, which was later leaked to the press, both the Poles and the Hungarians felt that Khrushchev was sending a message that the Soviet Union would now give its satellite countries more independence.

Sadly, this was not the case. After Poland and Hungary revolted, the Soviets clamped down on their control. Before long, the Soviet Union regained the upper hand in Poland, but the situation in Hungary got out of control.

In a revolt that lasted thirteen days, the Hungarians killed many Soviet officials and workers. The confronta-

*The support for Eisenhower was overwhelming
at the 1956 Republican convention.*

tion ended when the Soviet army took over, throwing many Hungarians in prison. By the end of the conflict, 50,000 Hungarians were killed. In November, Hungary appealed to the United Nations Security Council for help. The Soviet Union vetoed the proposal.

Eisenhower felt frustrated, but realized that the United States alone could not send troops into Hungary and stop the Soviets. He did, however, write to Soviet Premier Bulganin urging that the Soviets withdraw their troops from Hungary. The Soviets refused. Later, Ike offered asylum to thousands of Hungarians who came to the United States to escape the Soviet persecution.

Simultaneously, Eisenhower faced a more complicated dilemma, a crisis in the Middle East which took place in Egypt over the Suez Canal. This canal, one of the most important in the world, connects the Mediterranean and the Red Sea, two extremely busy waterways. Historically, the Suez Canal had always been open to world shipping. Soon after World War II, British troops were sent to parts of the canal to keep it open to international shipping, since the Egyptian government had threatened to nationalize it. Then in 1956, the Egyptians insisted that the British leave. Egyptian President Gamal Abdel Nasser had decided to make the Suez Canal part of Egypt. The British refused to pull out, and France sided with Britain.

Before long the situation in Egypt erupted into a shooting war. At this point, Eisenhower stepped in to keep the peace. He first contacted British Prime Minister Anthony Eden, asking him not to use military force. To complicate matters, the Israelis sided with Britain and France and made air attacks into Egypt. Egypt retaliated by attacking Israel. The eyes of the world were focused on the Middle East as an international war seemed imminent.

Eisenhower urged the United Nations to call for a cease-fire. After a heated debate, a cease-fire resolution

*Mamie Eisenhower shows her support during
Ike's second successful campaign in 1956.*

was approved, although Britain, France, and Israel opposed it. But even after the cease-fire, British and French troops attacked Egypt at Port Said on the Suez Canal.

In the final phase of this complicated situation, the Soviets sided with Egypt, and wanted the United States to do likewise. But Eisenhower refused.

The conflict ended abruptly when Britain and France agreed to the cease-fire. In this complex crisis, Ike had stepped in and stood up against two friendly countries— Britain and France—in order to gain world peace. Ike's policy fell under heavy criticism in England and France and, to some extent, in the United States also.

Since these two major world crises occurred just before the 1956 presidential election, Ike barely had time to campaign for re-election. But he was willing to stand on his record of the past four years. Most Americans felt that he had made progress during his first term and were willing to vote for him again. Appropriately, his campaign slogan was "Peace, Progress, and Prosperity."

After his re-election, Ike sincerely hoped that his second term in office would be easier than the first.

CHAPTER TWELVE

"The Winds of Change"

On a cold January day in 1957, as Dwight Eisenhower stood on a platform in front of the United States Capitol for his second inauguration, he said that ". . . all across the globe, there harshly blow the winds of change. We, in our good fortune, could never turn our backs to those winds or the peoples they touched."[1]

Ike knew he had to face changes at home and around the world. At home, many black Americans, after years of being treated like second-class citizens, were beginning to demand their civil rights. In Europe and elsewhere, the Soviet Union was becoming more aggressive. Adding to these challenges, Ike had to contend with a House and Senate controlled by the Democratic party. Ike realized that his second term as president would be more difficult than his first.

In the South, complications arose over the separation of black and white students in schools. In 1953 Eisenhower had appointed former California Governor Earl Warren chief justice of the Supreme Court. The next year, the Supreme Court made its historic decision declaring the separation of racial groups in schools unconstitutional.

People in the South strongly opposed this decision; there had always been racial separation in the southern schools. For many months, some of the southern states ignored the ruling.

Trouble erupted in the schools of Little Rock, Arkansas, which still practiced segregation. In September 1957, Arkansas Governor Orval Faubus called out units of the Arkansas National Guard to Central High School to "preserve peace and good order,"[2] and also to keep the black students from going to school in the formerly all-white high school. The school board backed the governor and declared that schools for white students were off limits to black students. They were directly defying the federal court order.

A crisis developed on the morning of September 23, when a mob of more than a thousand angry white people converged on Central High School, determined to keep the black students out. In spite of the mob, eight black children were able to enter the school through a side door. The mayor ordered the police to remove the black children from the school. After this development, the governor did nothing, thereby agreeing that the school remain segregated.

During this difficult time, Eisenhower had many telephone conversations with Governor Faubus urging him to uphold the federal law. After trouble erupted again, Ike issued a statement that Central High School had to become integrated. Despite this demand, on the following day the mob outside the school was larger than before, and the black students were denied the right to enter.

Finally, to end the disturbance, Eisenhower sent federal troopers to Little Rock. He wrote, "That afternoon 500 paratroops of the 101st Airborne Division from nearby Fort Campbell, Kentucky, arrived in Little Rock; another 500 moved in later the same day."[3]

Ike was upset about this episode and told a friend, "If the day comes when we can obey the orders of our courts only when we personally approve of them, the end of the American system, as we know it, will not be far off."[4]

Because Ike sent in the federal troops, black students were finally able to attend Central High School. But in spite of Ike's firm decision, he was criticized by many. Some people felt he should have called in the troops sooner, while many southerners opposed his interference in local problems.

The Little Rock incident disturbed Eisenhower a great deal, because he had always backed equal rights for all citizens. Later he invited Martin Luther King, Jr., and a delegation of other important people to meet with him at the White House. This was the first time that any group of black leaders had been asked to meet with the president.

Just a month after the incident in Little Rock, Americans were jolted by the firing of the world's first manmade satellite into orbit by the Soviet Union. This satellite was called "Sputnik," meaning traveling companion.

The launching of Sputnik caused alarm throughout the free world. Immediately, Americans began asking each other questions. How could the Russians have sent a satellite into space before the Americans? Were the Soviets really more advanced scientifically than any of the Western nations? Americans wondered why their schools were not teaching students more science and mathematics.

Ike was disturbed about the Soviet advance in space, and asked Congress to appropriate money to speed up the American space program.

In the midst of these difficulties, Ike experienced another health problem. He suffered a minor stroke. Fortunately, he recovered rapidly, and at the end of the year was able to attend the NATO conference in Paris.

Although Ike's health improved, 1958 turned out to

be a year that went from bad to worse. Trouble erupted in the Middle East when Egypt and Syria tried to instigate a revolt in Lebanon. President Chamoun of Lebanon called upon the United Nations and the United States for help. Eisenhower sent American marines to Lebanon to make sure that the government was not overthrown. This action was in compliance with the Eisenhower Doctrine, whereby the United States promised to protect the independence of any nation in the Middle East.

Then trouble developed in Cuba, when Communist Fidel Castro took over that nation. Ike and many other officials felt that the Soviet Union was trying to dominate the world. A Communist-controlled country only ninety miles from the United States was too close for comfort.

Just after Castro took over Cuba, a crisis developed in Berlin. Soviet Premier Khrushchev planned to sign a separate peace treaty with Communist East Germany, which would cancel the Four Power Agreement that gave the United States, Great Britain, France, and the Soviet Union access to Berlin. Ike had vivid memories of Berlin in flames at the end of World War II, and he wanted no more trouble there.

Discouraged over problems with the Soviets, Ike was surprised when, in July 1959, Premier Khrushchev decided to come to the United States. His visit was apparently not altogether Ike's idea. In fact, when Eisenhower heard that this invitation had been issued in his name, he became angry, saying that he had to "pay the penalty of going through with a meeting which would be 'a most unpleasant experience . . .' "5

In spite of his reluctance, Eisenhower gave Khrushchev a hearty welcome. Khrushchev was wined and dined everywhere he went, not only at the White House by President and Mrs. Eisenhower, but in New York and Los Angeles as well.

When Khrushchev arrived at the White House, he told Eisenhower that the Soviet Union wanted to have normal relations with the United States, saying, "We believe that you do not want war and we assume that you also believe this about us."

"I see no profit in mutual suicide."

Khrushchev continued, "The main thing is to establish trust. Probably we can't take each other's word at this time, but we must try to bring about trust. There is no other way. . . ."[6]

At this point, Ike truly hoped that he and the premier could reach some kind of understanding that would further peace between the two countries.

During his tour of the United States, Khrushchev visited a number of cities. He said New York was a "huge noisy city." Then, when he saw people on Park Avenue carrying signs that read, "Khrushchev, the Butcher of the Ukraine . . . Freedom for Hungary,"[7] he became irate.

Later in Los Angeles and Hollywood, people in the film industry gave a party in his honor, with Bob Hope, Henry Fonda, and Elizabeth Taylor attending. But when he saw people on the streets carrying signs similar to those he had seen in New York, he realized that many people did not like him or his country.

Ike wanted Khrushchev to finish his tour of the United States with a visit to Camp David, where the two heads of state could have private talks. Camp David was a presidential retreat in Maryland, named for Eisenhower's grandson, David.

As Ike was planning the Camp David meeting, the Soviet Union launched Sputnik II, undoubtedly to remind the world that the Russians were the first nation in space.

At the end of the Camp David visit, as Ike and Khrushchev talked of the Berlin crisis, Khrushchev promised to remove his threat to Berlin and said he hoped that a

In September 1959, Eisenhower and Soviet Premier Nikita Khrushchev arrive at Camp David for talks.

settlement could be reached. Eisenhower told Khrushchev that he was happy progress had been made, and suggested a Big Four summit meeting in December 1959. He also told Khrushchev that he would really like to make a trip to the Soviet Union in May. At this time, Ike felt quite friendly toward the premier.

On the last day at Camp David, as the two leaders were preparing a joint press statement, Khrushchev told Eisenhower that he wanted to omit any mention of an agreement on the Berlin situation. At this point, Ike exploded, saying, "This ends the whole affair—and I will go neither to a summit nor to Russia."[8] Ike could not believe that Khrushchev had changed his mind so soon.

Khrushchev explained that he did not want to issue a statement on Berlin until he returned to Moscow and first talked to the other Soviet leaders. After this explanation, Eisenhower agreed to wait.

Ike told Khrushchev that he was most anxious to go to Russia, saying, "I'll bring the whole family. You'll have more Eisenhowers there than you'll know what to do with."[9]

The night before Khrushchev returned to the Soviet Union, he appeared on American television. At the end of his speech, he said that he and the president had "very pleasant talks" at Camp David, and added, "I have no doubts whatever that the president sincerely desires an improvement of relations between our countries. . . ."[10]

Glad that Khrushchev's trip ended on a high note, Ike was confident that relations between the two countries were on the mend.

Later in the year, after the death of Secretary of State John Foster Dulles, Eisenhower decided to begin a program of personal diplomacy. He wanted to visit as many foreign countries as possible to speak out for world peace. Ike drew big crowds everywhere he went, mainly because he was remembered as a World War II hero. The countries Ike visited in December 1959 were Turkey, Pakistan, Afghanistan, India, Iran, Greece, Tunisia, France, Spain, and Morocco. Then in February 1960, he made a tour of South America.

Ike's one main hope was that he would be remembered as the president who brought a new era of peace to the world. He was working toward this goal as his last year as president approached.

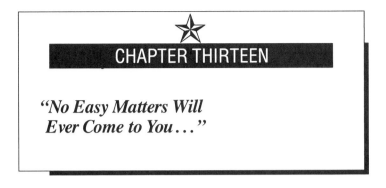

CHAPTER THIRTEEN

"No Easy Matters Will Ever Come to You..."

As Ike neared the end of his presidency, he truly hoped that relations between the United States and the Soviet Union had improved. Unfortunately, the last year of Ike's second term was marred by an ill-fated incident.

In the spring of 1960, he was preparing to attend the Big Four summit meeting between the United States, Great Britain, France, and the Soviet Union scheduled for May 16 in Paris. On May 1, Eisenhower received the news that one of the American U-2 planes had been shot down over the Soviet Union. The incident could not have occurred at a worse time, because May 1—May Day—is the Soviets' most important holiday, similar to our July 4.

After the Soviets had refused to cooperate with Eisenhower's Open Skies policy, the CIA persuaded Ike to approve the U-2 flights, which were resumed in April 1960. These planes took aerial photos over the Soviet Union. Ike had been told that if a pilot were shot down while on such a mission, there would be no chance of his surviving.

On May 1, Francis Gary Powers took off from an air base at Peshawar, Pakistan, on a flight over the Soviet

Union. Somewhere near Sverdlovsk, his plane was downed. After the news was first broadcast, Eisenhower and the United States government denied that the U-2 had flown over Soviet territory.

Then on May 6, Khrushchev appeared before the Supreme Soviet and announced that the uninjured pilot of the U-2 plane was being held, and that parts of his plane were to be put on display for the Russian people to view. After this development, Ike knew that the United States had to take responsibility for the flight.

On May 8, the *New York Times* headline read, "*U.S. Concedes Flight Over Soviet, Defends Search for Intelligence.*"[1]

At this point, the American people did not know what to think. Most Americans had never heard of the U-2 plane and did not know that the United States was flying spy planes. Americans had always trusted President Eisenhower; now they were completely confused when Ike first denied the U-2 flights and, later, after Khrushchev's accusations, admitted that the United States had flown the U-2 over the Soviet Union.

Ike was terribly upset about the situation. On May 9, after he had breakfast with some Republican Congressmen, he was so depressed about the U-2 affair that he said, "I would like to resign."[2]

Eisenhower later said that it was routine practice to deny responsibility for an embarrassing occurrence when there was even a small chance of being believed. But after the U-2 flight was a known fact, he realized he had to take full responsibility. He had never blamed anyone else for his actions.

At this time, some Americans criticized the president for admitting responsibility for the U-2 incident; others admired him for his forthright position. Assistant Secretary of State Douglas Dillon said, "He [Eisenhower] didn't like to blame other people. . . . He felt that more strongly than a civilian leader might have. He had this thing about honesty and that was the military tradition."3

Later Ike justified his use of the U-2 flights at a press conference, saying, "No one wants another Pearl Harbor. This means we must have knowledge of military forces and preparations around the world. . . .4

". . . This was the reason for my Open Skies proposal in 1955. . . . I shall bring up the Open Skies proposal again at Paris, since it is a means of ending concealment and suspicion. . . ."5

In spite of the U-2 incident, the Paris summit conference opened on May 16. As soon as French President Charles de Gaulle called the meeting to order, Soviet Chairman Khrushchev demanded to speak. Khrushchev was furious with Eisenhower and took back the invitation he had previously given to the president to visit the Soviet Union later in the year. He wanted Eisenhower to apologize for the U-2 incident and to promise that there would be no more flights over his country.

Because of the disagreement over the U-2 episode, the Paris conference broke up after two days.

Just after Power's plane was shot down, Eisenhower suspended any further U-2 flights. This was because the advanced technology of photographs from satellites had made the flights unnecessary. But Ike adamantly refused to apologize to Khrushchev. He steadfastly defended the use of the planes, believing that they had insured the safety of the United States and the free world. He felt that the Soviet Union had many spies within the United States and that we had a right to know as much about Soviet military bases as the Soviets did about ours.

After the conference broke up, Ike, sad and disappointed, returned home on May 20 in Air Force One. At Andrews Air Base, he walked down the ramp to meet

Mamie, who greeted him with tears in her eyes. Ike was on the verge of tears himself. *Newsweek* wrote: "This had been the biggest disappointment of his life and he made no attempt to hide it."[6]

Ike felt that bad luck had finally caught up with him. He knew that the U-2 affair had dealt a crushing blow to his crusade for world peace, and he realized there was little he could do about it.

After the failure of the Paris summit, the cold war with the Soviet Union began to escalate. At a United Nations meeting in 1960, Khrushchev lost his temper completely when the U-2 incident was brought up. He pounded his fist on the desk and even took his shoe off and banged it on the desk.

After Khrushchev's tirade, tensions between the two countries were worse than they had been for years. Many Americans feared that the Soviet Union would retaliate in some way for the U-2 affair, but the Soviets did not take any threatening action. In 1962, Francis Gary Powers, the U-2 pilot, was traded by the Soviet Union for the United States-held Soviet spy, Rudolf Abel.

In the last months of his presidency, a discouraged Eisenhower continued his personal diplomacy for world peace by traveling to the Far East, the Philippines, Korea, and Formosa. When he spoke publicly in these foreign countries, he told of the great need for better understanding between nations, for peace, and for nuclear disarmament. He had planned to visit Japan, but the Japanese canceled the trip because of Communist-inspired riots there.

In November 1960, Republicans Richard Nixon and Henry Cabot Lodge ran against Democrats John F. Kennedy and Lyndon Johnson in the presidential election. It turned out to be a close election, with the Democrats winning by only a small margin.

After the election, Ike was terribly disappointed because he had tried so very hard to bring peace to the world.

Eisenhower was impressed with President-elect John F. Kennedy (right) when he met with Kennedy at the White House following the 1960 election.

Although Eisenhower was frustrated with what he could not accomplish as president, many positive things did occur between 1952 and 1960. Here Ike signs the Alaska statehood bill.

He felt that the American people had rejected his policies. He said, ". . . I felt . . . as though eight years of work had been for naught."[7]

Shortly before he left office, Eisenhower invited President-elect Kennedy to the White House. Some of the advice that Ike gave the younger man was, "No easy matters will ever come to you. . . . If they're easy they will be settled at a lower level."[8]

Although from different political parties, Ike liked John Kennedy. He said, "I must confess to considerable gratification in this visit with the young man who was to be my successor. He conducted himself with unusual good taste. . . . I was struck by his pleasing personality, his concentrated interest, and his receptiveness."[9]

As Ike and Mamie prepared to leave the White House after eight years, they looked forward to retiring to their farm in Gettysburg. Filled with frustration over relations with the Soviet Union, Eisenhower's last year in office had been an extremely difficult one. Throughout this trying period, Eisenhower had always put the interests of the United States uppermost. Largely due to his effort, during his term of office the country had not been involved in a war. But in spite of his many achievements, Ike felt that his crusade for peace had not succeeded the way he had envisioned.

CHAPTER FOURTEEN

"We Kept the Peace..."

On January 17, 1961, Eisenhower made a televised farewell speech to the American people in which he tried to warn them of the dangers of a military buildup. He said that a huge military establishment was new to Americans, and that if the people were not careful, the arms industry would change their whole society. The citizens had to keep alert and try to combine a strong nation with peaceful goals.

Toward the end of his speech, he said, "... I confess that I lay down my official responsibilities in this field with a definite sense of disappointment. As one who has witnessed the horror and the lingering sadness of war, as one who knows that another war could utterly destroy this civilization ... I wish I could say tonight that a lasting peace is in sight ... so much remains to be done."[1]

On January 20, at the inauguration ceremony at the United States Capitol, Dwight D. Eisenhower turned the presidency over to John F. Kennedy. Kennedy was the youngest man ever to become president, and Eisenhower the oldest when he left office.

After the ceremony, as Ike and Mamie drove through the snow to their home in Gettysburg, Ike felt a certain relief that his eight years as president had come to an end.

The Eisenhowers had been looking forward to retiring on their farm. Mamie had designed a charming, comfortable home around a portion of an old wall and a Dutch oven, the only remaining part of the original 200-year-old home. Their 190-acre farm was stocked with a herd of Angus cattle, and there were horses for their grandchildren to ride.

As Ike had enjoyed every stage of his life, he now delighted in his retirement years—although he never completely retired, since he kept an office in nearby Gettysburg College, where he often worked from 7:30 A.M. to 4:00 P.M. writing books and answering correspondence. Many high government officials came to visit him. He also had telephone conversations with Presidents Kennedy and Johnson on several occasions.

Ike wrote about his years as president in a two-volume book titled *The White House Years, Mandate for Change* and *Waging Peace,* published in 1963 and 1965. In 1967, he wrote another book, *At Ease: Stories I Tell to Friends,* a reminiscence of his earlier years.

Ike spent part of his time relaxing and pursuing his hobbies. Since he was always a sports enthusiast, after retiring Ike played golf a great deal. He also had time for his other hobbies, including painting, fishing, and cooking. In his youth, Ike's mother had taught him how to cook, and now that he had the time, he was fond of barbecuing and making his favorite recipes of chili and chicken soup.

The Eisenhowers enjoyed frequent visits from John and Barbara and their four grandchildren, who discovered that the Gettysburg farm was an ideal place to have fun.

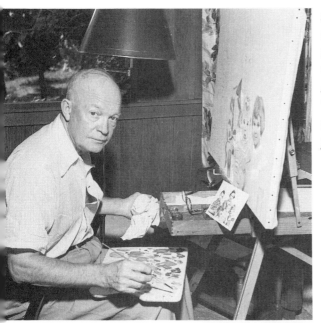

Ike enjoyed painting, but did not have much time for it while working. After he left the White House, he had the opportunity to pursue his hobbies.

Eisenhower instructs his grandson, David, on the fine art of putting.

*The Eisenhower family. For Ike,
his family and his country
had always been his life.*

When the winters became too cold in Gettysburg, Ike and Mamie flew to California and spent several months in Palm Springs in a home near the El Dorado Country Club, where Ike played golf almost every day. During their retirement years, Ike and Mamie finally had time to be together and appreciate each other.

Toward the end of his life, Eisenhower told a friend, when talking of his years as president, "We kept the peace. People ask how it happened—by God, it didn't just happen. I'll tell you that."[2] Ike was referring to ending the Korean War, and his many years of working for world peace. His only regret was that at the end of his presidency, relations between the United States and the Soviet Union were on the decline.

After a long illness, Dwight D. Eisenhower died in Washington at Walter Reed Hospital on March 28, 1969, at the age of seventy-nine. The last words Ike spoke to Mamie were, "I've always loved my wife. I've always loved my children. I've always loved my grandchildren. And I have always loved my country."[3] He was buried in a chapel at the Eisenhower Center in Abilene, Kansas.

Dwight D. Eisenhower will be remembered for his sincerity, his friendly concern for others, and his dedication to serving his country in an extremely perilous time. His congenial nature brought out the best in other people, making them want to achieve their highest goals. In the 1940s, many Europeans felt that Ike personified the true American—a trusted leader and a winner. In spite of all his accomplishments, Ike was a reluctant hero, a man who seemed to be unaware of his own greatness.

AFTERWORD

Of his presidency, Eisenhower wrote, "I had to admit to little success in making progress in global disarmament or in reducing the bitterness of the East-West struggle. . . . It seems incomprehensible that the men in the Kremlin can be ready to risk the destruction of their entire industrial fabric, their cities, their society and their ambitions rather than to enter into practical treaties, including systems of mutual inspection, that would immeasurably enrich their lives and those of all nations in the world.

"But though, in this, I suffered my greatest disappointment, it has not destroyed my faith that in the next generation, the next century, the next millennium, these things will come to pass." [1]

At a final press conference as president, Eisenhower was asked by a reporter: ". . . would you sum up for us your idea of what kind of a United States you would like your grandchildren to live in?"

The president replied that he hoped they might live "in a peaceful world . . . this means the effort always to raise the standards of our people in their spiritual, intellectual, [and] economic strength. That's what I would like to see them have." [2]

★ SOURCE NOTES

CHAPTER ONE

1. Relman Morin, *Dwight D. Eisenhower, A Gauge of Greatness* (New York, Simon & Schuster, 1969), 99.
2. *Ibid.*, 8.
3. *Ibid.*, 16.
4. Dwight D. Eisenhower, *In Review—Pictures I've Kept* (New York, Doubleday & Company, 1969), 2.
5. *Ibid.*, 2.
6. *Ibid.*, 5.
7. Merle Miller, *Ike the Soldier—As They Knew Him* (New York, P.G. Putnam, 1987), 87.
8. American Heritage Magazine and United Press International, *Eisenhower: An American Hero* (New York, American Heritage/Bonanza Books, 1969), 15.
9. Miller, *Ike the Soldier,* 87.
10. Dwight D. Eisenhower, *At Ease: Stories I Tell to Friends* (New York, Eastern Acorn Press, 1967), 16.
11. *Ibid.*, 97.
12. *Ibid.*, 40.

CHAPTER TWO

1. Dwight D. Eisenhower, *At Ease: Stories I Tell to Friends,* 102.
2. Merle Miller, *Ike the Soldier—As They Knew Him,* 130.
3. Eisenhower, *At Ease,* 4.
4. *Ibid.*

5. Miller, 19.
6. Eisenhower, *At Ease,* 8.
7. Eisenhower, *In Review—Pictures I've Kept,* 15.
8. Miller, 125.
9. *Ibid.*
10. *Ibid.,* 31.
11. Eisenhower, *In Review,* 15.
12. *Ibid.,* 18.
13. Miller, 43.
14. Relman Morin, *Dwight D. Eisenhower,* 25.

CHAPTER THREE

1. D.D. Eisenhower, *In Review—Pictures I've Kept,* 19.
2. *Ibid.,* 19.
3. Merle Miller, *Ike the Soldier—As They Knew Him,* 143.
4. Eisenhower, *Waging Peace,* 175.
5. Miller, 146.
6. *Ibid.*
7. Eisenhower, *In Review,* 20–21.
8. Miller, 149.
9. *Ibid.*
10. Stephen E. Ambrose, *Eisenhower—Soldier, General of the Army, President-Elect* (New York, Simon & Schuster, 1983), 59.
11. *Ibid.,* 65.
12. William E. Longgood, *A Pictorial Biography—Ike* (New York, Time-Life Books, 1969), 29.
13. Eisenhower, *In Review,* 26.
14. Eisenhower, *At Ease,* 181.

CHAPTER FOUR

1. Stephen E. Ambrose, *Eisenhower—Soldier,* 75.
2. *Ibid.,* 77.
3. *Ibid.,* 78.
4. *Ibid.,* 79.
5. *Ibid.*
6. D.D. Eisenhower, *In Review,* 32.
7. *Ibid.*
8. Merle Miller, *Ike the Soldier,* 260.
9. Ambrose, 94.
10. Ambrose, 93.
11. Eisenhower, *In Review,* 35.
12. Ambrose, 112.

13. Eisenhower, *In Review,* 38.
14. Robert H. Ferrell, ed., *The Eisenhower Diaries* (New York, W.W. Norton & Company, 1981), 37.
15. Ambrose, 119.

CHAPTER FIVE

1. Stephen E. Ambrose, *Eisenhower—Soldier,* 120.
2. *Ibid.,* 121.
3. William E. Longgood, *A Pictorial Biography—Ike,* 45–46.
4. Ambrose, 130.
5. *Encyclopedia Britannica,* 1969 Edition, Vol. 5, 750.
6. Ambrose, 131.
7. D.D. Eisenhower, *Crusade in Europe* (Garden City, N.Y., Doubleday & Company, 1948), 14.
8. Merle Miller, 340.
9. Eisenhower, *In Review,* 42.
10. Merle Miller, 340.

CHAPTER SIX

1. Robert H. Ferrell, ed., *The Eisenhower Diaries,* 94.
2. *Ibid.,* 91.
3. D.D. Eisenhower, *In Review,* 52.
4. D.D. Eisenhower, *Letters to Mamie,* ed. John S.D. Eisenhower (New York, Doubleday & Company, 1978), 128.
5. Stephen E. Ambrose, *Eisenhower—Soldier,* 260.
6. *Ibid.*
7. *Ibid.*

CHAPTER SEVEN

1. Relman Morin, *Dwight D. Eisenhower,* 97.
2. D.D. Eisenhower, *Crusade in Europe,* 225.
3. *Ibid.,* 239.
4. *Ibid.,* 245.
5. Morin, 100.
6. Morin, 99.
7. *Ibid.,* 102.

CHAPTER EIGHT

1. D.D. Eisenhower, *Letters to Mamie,* 190.
2. Stephen E. Ambrose, *Eisenhower—Soldier,* 312.

3. Robert Ferrell, *Eisenhower Diaries,* 94.
4. Eisenhower, *Crusade in Europe,* 279.
5. Eisenhower, *In Review,* 78.
6. Eisenhower, *Crusade in Europe,* 350.
7. *Ibid.,* 354–5.
8. Ambrose, 372.
9. *Ibid.,* 371.
10. Eisenhower, *Letters to Mamie,* 227.
11. Stephen E. Ambrose, *Ike—Abilene to Berlin* (New York, Harper & Row, 1973), 185.

CHAPTER NINE

1. D.D. Eisenhower, *Crusade in Europe,* 380.
2. *Ibid.,* 408–9.
3. *Ibid.,* 409.
4. Merle Miller, *Ike the Soldier,* 771.
5. Stephen E. Ambrose, *Ike—Abilene to Berlin,* 190.
6. *The Historical Encyclopedia of World War II* (New York, Greenwich House, 1977), 224.
7. Miller, 776.
8. *Ibid.,* 777.
9. *Ibid.*
10. Eisenhower, *Crusade in Europe,* 426.
11. *Ibid.*
12. Miller, 778.
13. *Ibid.,* 779.
14. Eisenhower, *Crusade in Europe,* 428.
15. Ambrose, *Ike—Abilene to Berlin,* 203.
16. Eisenhower, *At Ease,* 390.

CHAPTER TEN

1. D.D. Eisenhower, *At Ease,* 388.
2. Alfred Steinberg, *Dwight David Eisenhower* (New York, G.P. Putnam's Sons, 1967), 159.
3. Jules Archer, *Battlefield President, Dwight D. Eisenhower* (New York, Julian Messner, 1967), 120.
4. Eisenhower, *In Review,* 99.
5. Archer, 122.
6. Eisenhower, *In Review,* 113.
7. *Ibid.*
8. *Ibid.,* 116.

CHAPTER ELEVEN

1. William E. Longgood, *A Pictorial Biography—Ike,* 86.
2. *Ibid.*
3. *Ibid.*
4. D.D. Eisenhower, *In Review,* 119.
5. *Ibid.,* 122.
6. Jules Archer, *Battlefield President,* 138.
7. Eisenhower, *In Review,* 126.
8. D.D. Eisenhower, *The White House Years, Mandate for Change* (New York, Doubleday & Company, 1963), 105.
9. Eisenhower, *In Review,* 141.
10. Michael Beschloss, *Mayday* (New York, Harper & Row, 1986), 100.
11. *Ibid.,* 104.
12. *Ibid.,* 101–2.
13. *Ibid.,* 103.
14. *Ibid.,* 105.

CHAPTER TWELVE

1. D.D. Eisenhower, *The White House Years, Waging Peace* (New York, Doubleday & Company, 1965), 103.
2. Eisenhower, *In Review,* 180.
3. *Ibid.,* 182.
4. Eisenhower, *Waging Peace,* 175.
5. Michael Beschloss, *Mayday,* 177.
6. *Ibid.,* 190–1.
7. *Ibid.,* 198.
8. Eisenhower, *In Review,* 210.
9. Beschloss, 213.
10. *Ibid.*

CHAPTER THIRTEEN

1. Michael Beschloss, *Mayday,* 250.
2. *Ibid.,* 254.
3. *Ibid.,* 252.
4. *Ibid.,* 265.
5. *Ibid.*
6. *Ibid.,* 304.
7. D.D. Eisenhower, *In Review,* 228.
8. Lonnelle Aikeman, *The Living White House* (Washington, D.C., The White House Historical Association, 1970), 133.
9. Eisenhower, *In Review,* 233.

CHAPTER FOURTEEN

1. Full speech in *Los Angeles Times,* Jan. 18, 1961.
2. Michael Beschloss, *Mayday,* 388.
3. American Heritage Magazine, *Eisenhower: An American Hero,* 135.

AFTERWORD

1. Michael Beschloss, *Mayday,* 343.
2. D.D. Eisenhower, *In Review,* 234.

BIBLIOGRAPHY

Aikman, Lonnelle. *The Living White House.* Washington, D.C.: The White House Historical Association, 1987.

Ambrose, Stephen E. Vol. 1, *Eisenhower—Soldier, General of the Army, President-Elect (1890–1951)*, Vol. 2, *The President.* New York: Simon & Schuster, 1983, 1984.

Ambrose, Stephen E. *Ike—Abilene to Berlin.* New York: Harper & Row, 1973.

American Heritage Magazine and United Press International. *Eisenhower: An American Hero.* New York: American Heritage/Bonanza Books, 1969.

Archer, Jules. *Battlefield President, Dwight D. Eisenhower.* New York: Julian Messner, 1967.

Berding, Andrew. *Foreign Affairs and You.* New York: Doubleday & Company, 1962.

Beschloss, Michael R. *Mayday.* New York: Harper & Row, 1986.

Bradley, Omar. *A Soldier's Story.* New York: Henry Holt & Company, 1951.

Butcher, Harry C. *My Three Years with Eisenhower, 1942–45.* New York: Simon & Schuster, 1946.

David, Lester and Irene. *Ike and Mamie—The Story of the General and His Lady.* New York: G.P. Putnam's Sons, 1955.

Durant, John and Alice. *Pictorial History of American Presidents.* New York: A.S. Barnes & Company, 1955.

Eisenhower, David. *Eisenhower at War 1943–45.* New York: Random House, 1986.

Eisenhower, Dwight D. *At Ease: Stories I Tell to Friends.* New York: Eastern Acorn Press, 1967.

Eisenhower, Dwight D. *Crusade in Europe.* Garden City, N.Y.: Doubleday & Company, 1948.

Eisenhower, Dwight D. *In Review—Pictures I've Kept.* Garden City, N.Y.: Doubleday & Company, 1969.

Eisenhower, Dwight D. *Letters to Mamie.* Edited by John S.D. Eisenhower. Garden City, N.Y.: Doubleday & Company, 1978.

Eisenhower, Dwight D. *The White House Years,* Volume 1, *Mandate for Change (1953–56)*: Volume 2, *Waging Peace.* Garden City, N.Y.: Doubleday & Company, 1963, 1965.

Eisenhower, John S.D. *Strictly Personal.* Garden City, N.Y.: Doubleday & Company, 1974.

Encyclopedia Britannica. Chicago, London: William Benton, Publisher, 1969 Edition.

Faber, Doris. *Dwight Eisenhower.* New York: Abelard-Schuman, 1977.

Ferrell, Robert H., ed. *The Eisenhower Diaries.* New York: W.W. Norton & Company, 1981.

Longgood, William E. *A Pictorial Biography—Ike.* New York: Time-Life Books, 1969.

McCann, Kevin. *Man from Abilene.* Garden City, N.Y.: Doubleday & Company, 1952.

Miller, Merle. *Ike the Soldier—As They Knew Him.* New York: G.P. Putnam's Sons, 1987.

Morin, Relman. *Dwight D. Eisenhower, A Gauge of Greatness.* New York: Simon & Schuster, 1969.

Pinkley, Virgil, with James F. Scheer. *Eisenhower Declassified.* Old Tappan, N.J.: Fleming H. Revell Company, 1979.

Smith, S.E., ed. *The United States Navy in World War II.* New York: William Morrow & Company, 1966.

Steinberg, Alfred. *Dwight David Eisenhower.* New York: G.P. Putnam's Sons, 1967.

Summersby, Kay. *Eisenhower Was My Boss.* New York: Prentice-Hall, Inc., 1948.

The Historical Encyclopedia of World War II. New York: Greenwich House, 1977.

★ FOR FURTHER READING

Ambrose, Stephen E. *Abilene to Berlin.* New York: Harper & Row, 1973.

Archer, Jules. *Battlefield President, Dwight D. Eisenhower.* New York: Julian Messner, 1967.

Beschloss, Michael R. *Mayday.* New York: Harper & Row, 1986.

Eisenhower, Dwight D. *At Ease: Stories I Tell to Friends.* New York: Eastern Acorn Press, 1967.

Eisenhower, Dwight D. *In Review—Pictures I've Kept.* New York: Doubleday & Company, 1969.

Longgood, William E. *A Pictorial Biography—Ike.* New York: Time-Life Books, 1969.

McCann, Kevin. *Man From Abilene.* Garden City, N.Y.: Doubleday & Company, 1952.

INDEX

Gettysburg, 40, 42, 107

Harding, Gladys, 29, 33
Harriman, Averell, 104
Hazlett, Everett, 24
Himmler, Heinrich, 98–99
Hitler, Adolf, 55, 83, 88, 98
Hungarian revolt of 1956, 122,
    124

Jodl, General, 99
Johnson, Lyndon, 138, 142

Kennedy, John F., 138, *139*, 140,
    141, 142
Khrushchev, Nikita, 120–21, 122,
    130–31, *132*, 133, 136, 137,
    138
King, Martin Luther, Jr., 129
Korean War, 113, 115, *116*, 117,
    119
Krueger, General, 57

Lebanon crisis of 1958, 130
Lee, Tex, 58
Leigh-Mallory, Trafford, 79
Lodge, Henry Cabot, 110, 111,
    138

MacArthur, Douglas, 45, 50–52,
    54, 113–14
McAuliffe, Anthony, 90
McCarthy, Joseph, 119–20
Marshall, George C., 45, 48,
    59, 60, 61, 64, *67*, 68, 84,
    85
Merrifield, Wesley, 19
Montgomery, Bernard "Monty,"
    65, 68, 81, 86, 88, 91, 97,
    100–101
Mussolini, Benito, 69

Nasser, Gamal Abdel, 124
Nixon, Richard, 114, 122, 138

Normandy invasion (OVERLORD):
    Allied agreement on, 70
    Allied victory, 81, 83
    D-Day, 13, 15, 77, 79–81,
        82
    Ike named as commander, 71
    preparations for, 71–72, 74,
        75–76, 77, *78*, 79
North Atlantic Treaty Organization
    (NATO), 109–10, 111

Open Skies policy, 121, 122, 137
OVERLORD. *See* Normandy
    invasion

Patton, George, 43, 64–65, 68,
    85, 89, 91, 93–94, 96–97, 98,
    105, 106
Pearson, Drew, 57
Pershing, John J., 45, 49
Powers, Francis Gary, 135–36,
    138
Presidential elections:
    1952, 110–12, 113–15
    1956, 122, *123*, *125*, 126

Quezon, Manuel, 50, 51–52

Randolph, Norman, 42
Rhee, Syngman, 117
Rommel, Erwin, 65, 66, 81, 83,
    88
Roosevelt, Franklin D., 15, 50,
    56, 58, 61, 64, 68, 69, 70, 71,
    77, 80, 96, 98
Rundstedt, Gerd von, 81, 83

Smith, Walter Bedell, 59, 69, 99
Space program, 129
Sputnik satellites, 129, 131
Stalin, Joseph, 77, 96, 104, 122
Stassen, Harold, 114
Stevenson, Adlai, 114
Suez crisis of 1956, 124, 126

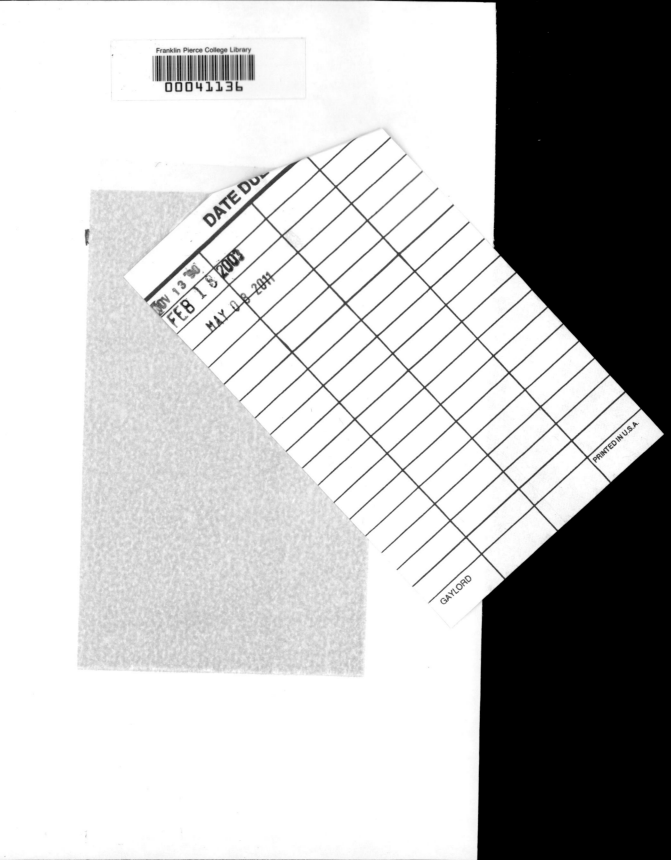